WORLDING
A GUIDE FOR CREATORS IN CHANGING TIMES

IAN CHENG

Foreword by Venkatesh Rao

First print edition published by cosmogenesis 2026

WORLDING: A Guide for Creators in Changing Times was originally published as an e-book under the title *Emissary's Guide to Worlding* by Metis Suns, New York

Edited by Ben Vickers
Design by Kathryn Politis
Cover art by Ian Cheng & Eden Rose Cheng
Typeset in Averia Serif Libre
Printed in the UK by Bell & Bain Ltd

EU GPSR Authorised Representative
LOGOS EUROPE
9 rue Nicolas Poussin, 17000,
La Rochelle, France
contact@logoseurope.eu

1 3 5 7 9 10 8 6 4 2

cosmogenesis.world
ISBN: 9781068765728

CONTENTS

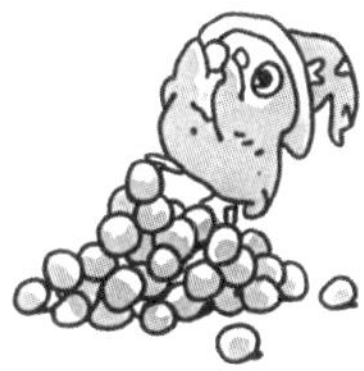

PREFACE: LOTS AND LOTS OF LITTLE WORLDS

The genesis of this book was *Emissaries Guide to Worlding* (EGTW), a catalog for my 2018 exhibition *Emissaries* at the Serpentine. At the time, I was obsessed with the question: could I make an artwork that doesn't just last, but lives? The experience of creating simulated worlds—inhabited by virtual agents evolving on their own—was rewiring my approach to art-making. A new mode was emerging. I wanted to capture this shift and put a name to it as a distinct creative activity: Worlding.

In 2019, I expanded the EGTW catalog into a full-length e-book that could stand alone from the *Emissaries Trilogy* artwork that framed the original book. The subject of worlding deserved a usable playbook, one rooted in the psychology of the artist. I detailed the interplay of four creative modes—masks—that the artist adopts: the Cartoonist, the Hacker, the Director, and the Emissary. I highlighted the role of the Emissary, the most unpracticed and unsexy mask, but the most vital for Worlding. It's the part of a creator dedicated to seeing an artwork as a living organism, and nurturing its long-term flourishing, as one would for a pet, a child, a house, or a garden.

That same year, Venkatesh Rao invited me to riff on worlding with him on his blog Ribbonfarm. That became *Worlding Raga,* a series of posts exploding these ideas in speculative directions. For me, this was an early signal that Worlding might have resonance beyond the domain of contemporary art.

But the truth is, in 2019, worlding was something I thought about more than something I put into practice. I was writing about worlding as an activity applicable to a creator in any arena, but I hadn't lived it outside the narrow frame of art-making. And I quietly avoided one of my own core criteria for worlding: that to make a world come alive, it must be in a feedback loop with real people who choose to inhabit it.

Feedback with reality. What a pain. This is the aspect of worlding that continues to haunt me: its attempt to address creative endeavors that engage with real stakes—real people, real markets, real pains, real energy—as the primary source of creative tension. Not for the sake of performative shock or attention farming. But because an engagement with real stakes means touching the gnarly complexity of things, testing wishful beliefs with what actually works, opening yourself to unambiguous failure and learning to interpret the information in it. Worlding is a way of doing creative work that becomes synonymous with navigating life itself.

A lot of life has happened since the first publication of EGTW. I've become a dad to two kiddos. I've developed a lifelong obsession with jiu-jitsu. I've founded a startup building AI for families. Never before have I submitted myself to so much unwishful, unrelenting feedback. These are hard worlds. Stressful. Often annoying. But they grip reality, animate it with meaning, and drag me along with it. I've discovered that tending to them has made life inexhaustibly satisfying.

Over these dizzying years, I've heard from hundreds of people adapting the ideas of worlding to their own domain. Artists, game designers, protocol builders, teachers, architects, technologists, strategists, founders, families. People trying to navigate the messiness of building living systems with long horizons. I've learned from them that the appetite for worlding is a response to two patterns: First, that the complaint-driven playbook taught in school over the last decades is a losing script. Second, that energy really matters in the success of creative work today—that some projects seem to just come alive, in the literal sense, becoming self-perpetuating flywheels of energy, begetting more projects, more people, and more feedback. Worlding is the name for doing more of that.

This book, *Worlding: A Guide for Creators in Changing Times,* published by cosmogenesis, collects my writings on worlding. I've made minimal updates to reflect terminology beyond art and artists, while keeping the text's roaming iterations intact as they were written seven years ago. More than I could have envisioned, *Worlding* is for the creator who is awake to the realities of our tribulatory times: The collapse of institutions. The untenable expense of daily life. Instant access to mass networks of attention. The abundance of technological capability. If you see this shitstorm as a creative opportunity—against the tired instincts to retreat from it or to critically illustrate it—this book is for you.

And if worlding all seems very serious, it's because it is an art that has the potential to be life changing. But I'd preface one thing I've re-learned from my own kids: the practice of any art begins with a spirit of play. Worlding is no exception. In play, feedback with reality is the whole damn point. You just try things. You poke reality and see what pokes back. You converge on more of what begets energy AND what interests you. A magic circle forms—the beginnings of a little world—and a corner of reality suddenly feels grippable. As incumbent Old Worlds war with each other and compete for your soul, you crowd their hold by worlding little worlds. Lots and lots of little worlds. Somewhere in there is the place you will make a life out of.

Here's a map:
You survive reality by inhabiting Worlds. (Life begins here)
You question reality by rejecting Worlds. (But don't get stuck here)
You play with reality by creating lots and lots of little worlds. (Worlding begins here)
You dent reality by nurturing worlds into Worlds. (You make a life here)

Live to World! World to live!
Ian Cheng
February 7th, 2026

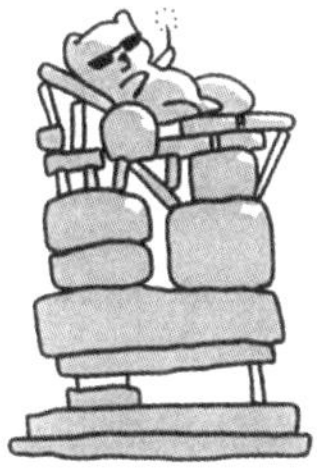

FOREWORD

A quarter-century ago, as a young graduate student studying control theory, I realized my temperament was naturally at odds with a fundamental dogma of my field: *when studying a system, start with the simplest possible toy model.*[1]

My problem, I realized, was that I really enjoyed complicating things. I didn't know it yet, but I was itching to use computers to conjure and play with entire high-fidelity worlds, not pen-and-paper math to poke at low-fidelity shards. To use a word I would learn from Ian Cheng twenty years later, I was interested in *worlding,* not theorem-proving.

My field demanded a simplicity bias. I have a complicatedness bias. In defiance of Occam's razor, I like to multiply entities needlessly.

My bias isn't arbitrary contrarianism though. The principle of ontological parsimony that serves us so well in the pursuit of truth by reductionism does not work quite so well

[1] Since control theory is a highly mathematical field — a cynic would say a field for applied mathematicians who couldn't cut it as pure mathematicians — modeling and solving have very rigorous meanings, which leads to simple being roughly equivalent to toy. In fact, "toy model" is used interchangeably with "simple model." While models and solutions to problems in control theory are often wonderfully and satisfyingly legible, with beautiful mathematical properties like provable stability and convergence, they are rarely practical. In far too many ways, they are too simple.

when working with the phenomenology of emergence. The truths buried beneath classic epics, vast cinematic and video game universes, enormous AI models, bewildering on-chain games, and grand political hyperstitions, require a taste for complexity, multiplicity, variety, and particularity. To engage in worlding, we need not a parsimony principle, but a *profligacy* principle.

There's one within easy reach: Alan Kay famously noted that to use computers well, we must "waste transistors." By extension, we might say, to world well, we must *waste entities.* This is the profligacy principle I suspect we need.

This book, arguably, is about how to waste entities. How to tell stories with thousands of characters and objects where, by the austere ethos of the pre-digital age, mere dozens might do. How to spawn and work with infinite variations on a theme, where we might previously have sought a single distilled canonical archetype.

In grad school, if a model or problem statement felt too simple, my instinct (against the best advice of my professors) was to complicate it until it felt like it was at the right resolution. For me, the problem with starting simple and trying to add complications systematically was that the simple models didn't really scale. At least not systematically. You had to rebuild models from new first principles at every new scale and scope. Simpler models at best served to refine your intuitions and supply some building blocks along the way.

And reductionists tend not to try at all. When working in reductionist modes, you typically never get to complicated models of practical interest at all. Instead, you add angels-on-a-pinhead theological refinements. Practicality ends up a casualty of the reductionist bias toward simplicity.

The simplicity bias has many such casualties. How you retreat from simplicity is a function of which casualty you care about. That determines which aspect of it you *abandon,* and *how* you complicate matters.

Practicality is the most obvious casualty, which causes the industrial discipline of control engineering to diverge from academic control theory by adding important kinds of textural richness and abandoning mathematical aesthetics.[2] Political ambition is another casualty, which historically led to the child field of cybernetics forking away from control theory by expanding scale and scope of application to large-scale social systems, and abandoning empirical rigor and (through extreme abstraction), what we might call *ontological fidelity.*[3]

For me, as a young researcher circa 2000, the casualty that concerned me was *interestingness.* Too-simple models are boring, just as too-simple toys are boring for kids past a certain age.

Back then, it struck me that the simplicity bias of my professors, all a generation or two older than me, was anchored to simple toys even a five-year-old would tire of in hours. They worked with such toy models not because they found them genuinely interesting, but because the adult research

[2] Control engineering is basically the art of adding enough ugly complications and messiness to the toy models studied by the theorists so that they become usable in practice, sacrificing many mathematical properties prized by theorists along the way. Practicalities that elude elegant mathematization (and are therefore only reluctantly engaged with by theorists), such as static friction, saturations, delays, discretization, hysteresis, aliasing, and unpleasant patterns of noise and disturbance, enter into consideration. And engineers respond with a vast array of hacks, some of which theorists occasionally deign to study. If you're lucky, those hacks will not entirely erase the upsides of all the elegance the theorists worked so hard to supply.

[3] Cybernetics has historically concerned itself with large-scale systems with social elements, such as cities, industries, and even the entire planet. It was founded in the 1960s by a few rebel pioneers of control theory. Cybernetics abandoned the rigor and empiricism of control theory, which its customers in the worlds of policy-making and management weren't asking for anyway, leading to many infamous failures of prophecy. More importantly, cybernetics also abandons ontological fidelity. Instead of dealing with toy models of relatively real things like aircraft, missiles, and pendulums, it models the world with thin abstractions like "stocks" and "flows" that abstract away much of the detail that is of interest to complicatedness-nerds like me. Cybernetics makes extensive use of computers too, but in a very different way that reveals the age of the field. Cybernetics' models look nothing like video games. Instead, they look like the kinds of non-interactive models that used to run on mainframes and minicomputers through the 1970s. Models that strip away the "skin" of reality to reveal what the model builders believe, based on little more than auteur opinions, to be the "bones."

tools they had mastered could not handle more complex toys. For instance, the system most often used as a pedagogical example in control theory, from undergraduate to PhD levels, is the inverted pendulum on a cart. As a toy, this system corresponds to a broomstick a kid might try to balance on their palm. As a model of practical engineering systems, it corresponds to messy problems like stabilizing a rocket. But neither broomsticks, nor rockets, arguably, constitute *worlds.* That's not enough entities.

My generation was the first to be raised on video games. Not surprisingly, many in my generation of PhDs began drawing on video game experiences rather than physical toys when it came to thinking about "toy models" for research.

As a result, not only was my work based primarily on simulation results rather than formal theorems (it took some time for my advisor to get on board with the idea that simulations could count as research), the simulations were of significantly more complex systems than pendulums on carts. In my later postdoctoral research, I abandoned formal theorems and proofs entirely, and built toy research worlds that were unabashedly inspired by video games. While you *could* write down equations describing these worlds, they were typically far too complex to analyze with theorems. And that was never the point.

It made much more sense to code up the models, articulate and instrument them, and then... play them like video games. The logged data—evolutionary traces of things that looked like small but complete worlds, and required hundreds of variables to describe—turned into research papers. We weren't yet in the age of research-by-the-GPU-truckload that we are in today, but we were starting down that path.

While the previous generation of researchers in my field had used simulation tools to effectively automate tedious pen-and-paper math for systems about as complex as pendulums on carts, my generation began using simulation as a tool to probe systems that were too complex to be tractably modeled on paper. Our models had a greater number and variety of moving parts, with more complex interactions, than anything our predecessors in the field had handled.

Alongside methods, *goals* changed.

Like control engineers in industry, I found myself adding textural richness, but in service of interestingness rather than practicality. And unlike them, I found I did not have to sacrifice mathematical elegance to do so. Like cyberneticians, I found myself adding scale and scope, but in service of interestingness rather than political ambition. And I found I did not have to sacrifice empiricism or ontological fidelity to do so.

It felt as though, by pursuing interestingness, I was getting some sort of free lunch. It was, in fact, the same free lunch that has been powering the world for decades: Moore's Law. Solving for interestingness taps into the abundances of computing in a way solving for practicality or political ambition does not. The pursuit of interestingness is almost *necessary* for operating by the profligacy principle.

Worlding, in the sense that Ian explores in this volume, is a young activity born of digital abundances. What Vannevar Bush called the endless frontier of science has transformed, thanks to computing, into an eternal free lunch, for those able to cultivate the literacies of profligacy required to access it.

Abundance, in the context of worlding, is best understood as a condition that offers *reliable renewability of purpose and meaning.* To use James Carse's term, it is a condition that underwrites the infinite game; a condition that will always offer a way to continue playing. So long as you're willing and able to multiply entities needlessly.

With great power comes great responsibility. The profligacy principle opens up easy pathways to degeneracy. To avoid them, you need a range of worlding literacies, ranging from technical to moral. These take effort to acquire and practice.

Which means you can be bad at worlding, and many people are.

The DC universe is as bad as the Marvel and Star Wars universes are good. For every startling on-chain art or gaming project, there are a thousand shitcoins and NFT grifts. For every intriguing use of generative AI to make art, we can point to megatons of slop that consumed gigawatts of energy to no interesting end. For every generative political narrative that taps into a vein of flourishing, there are a thousand paranoid cults built around hyperstitions of resentment.

Some of the bad worlding, of course, is a result of the wastefulness inherent in the profligacy principle. As Rick Sanchez notes in *Rick and Morty,* "The universe is basically an animal. It grazes on the ordinary. It creates infinite idiots just to eat them."

But a good deal of bad worlding is attributable to basic illiteracy. As a species, we are just beginning to learn how to world well.

Computing infrastructures are spawning worlds faster than we are learning to live well in them. Worlds governed by strange new rules. Worlds equipped not just with their own sensoria (whether virtual, augmented, or mixed), but with their own economies, epistemologies, and ontologies. Worlds with latent hyperstitional potentials capable of reshaping reality itself.

It is tempting to regard this multiversal worlding frenzy as a delusional mass retreat from reality, a belief that is in fact false. Succumbing to this false belief leads to a profoundly false dichotomy.

In 2004, for example, an unnamed Bush administration official famously declared, "We're an empire now, and when we act, we create our own reality," dismissing in the process the "reality-based community" that shaped the opposed Democrat posture, which was then beginning its long descent into its current haplessness. Now, two decades later, politics worldwide seems hopelessly trapped in a global version of the false dichotomy.

Versions can be found in other domains. In an essay popular with literary types, *Against Worldbuilding,* and follow-on essays, the novelist Lincoln Michel falls into the same trap as the Bush official, belaboring a distinction between "hard world-building" through on-the-nose rules-based construction, and "world conjuring" through gesture and suggestion. Setting aside the underlying literary-over-genre craft conceits, the dichotomy here is quite obviously an artifact of attachment to profligacy-limited, parsimonious textual modes. To build a good video game or extended universe movie franchise, clearly you must do a good deal of *both* hard world-building and world-conjuring.

Fortunately, unlike in politics, in literature, writers are beginning to escape this trap. The seminal science fiction novel *There Is No Antimemetics Division,* which emerged from the online worlding community known as SCP, cheerfully manages to build and conjure at the same time.

It took me a decade past grad school to finally break out of this dichotomy myself. The result was a 2014 essay, *On the Design of Escaped Realities,* in which I argued that not only do you not have to choose between reality and worlding agency, worlding is the only way you can access reality at all.

The better you are at worlding, the more closely you *approach* reality. The most escapist worlds we inhabit are not our newest digital worlds, but our oldest. Technological evolution over millennia, far from alienating us from reality, has in fact, brought us into increasingly deeper communion with it. The worlds conjured by ancient religions gave way to the imagined communities of nationalist mythologies conjured up by newspapers and television. And these are giving way today to worlds that require enormous computing power to sustain, but offer enormous amounts of agency in return.

Living in reality takes a *lot* of literal work. Building complex worlds to approach reality in, is work measurable in gigawatts.

What is surprising is that this is surprising to people. After all, we journey into outer space not on the backs of mythical beasts imagined by ancient religions, but in extraordinarily complex machines that reflect an extraordinarily complex understanding of the realities of space travel. An understanding that even kids can now access to some degree, through video games like *Kerbal Space Program,* without being constrained by a lack of advanced mathematical training.

As A. N. Whitehead famously noted, "Civilization advances by extending the number of important operations which we can perform without thinking of them."

Worlding, we might say, is the art and science of living in realities where the number of such operations is increasing exponentially. And in this book, Ian has laid out some of the earliest lessons we have learned about how to do it well.

Venkatesh Rao
August, 2025

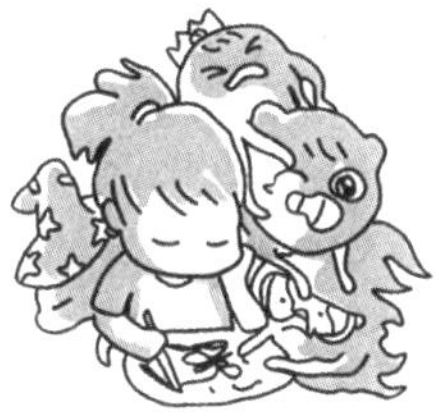

INTRODUCTION

From an early age, my mom would take me movie hopping on weekends at the shopping mall cinema in the San Fernando Valley. She would buy us matinée tickets for the first show in the morning and we'd hop into four or five different movies until dinner. The transition between theater rooms always made me anxious. I was afraid we'd get caught sneaking into the next movie and have to endure the shame of being kicked out. But my mom savored this game. She would instruct me to go to the restroom, remove an outer layer and mess up my hair. I'd come out to see her transformed in glasses, a tied-up bun, and wearing a jacket. On our journey to the next theater room, she would risk asking an usher for directions with played urgency, or take her time browsing snacks at the concession stand. I'd nag her to keep moving. A wave of relief would come over me every time we made it inside the next theater and sank into our seats. We had beaten the odds, enough to play again. The movies themselves, whatever their content, were a zone of stability before the next hop between theaters.

Later, when my parents were between jobs, they would buy a lotto ticket every Sunday with the same six lucky numbers. For them, the California Lottery was just a little game to satisfy a superstitious itch, not an actual answer to employment. My dad did the math: the odds of winning were 300 million to one. Smaller than getting struck by lightning three times in your life. I'd ask myself, is luck on our side this week? A mysterious voice would answer: 'count the birds on the wire and all will transpire!' Every Sunday I'd ritualistically count the birds outside my window, tune into the live number drawing, and bet the universe that this evil random game might resolve something. And every Sunday, when the right numbers never came, I'd demand that the voice explain itself. But it only spoke nonsense until my anxiety built back up to next week's roll of the game.

In hindsight, I yearned for some tutorial that might have been called Navigating the Chasm. If I had known to see the transitional gap between theaters as an opportunity to inhabit a role and choose the next chapter of my day, I would have learned to enjoy the thrill of creating choices. And if I had learned to hallucinate that the feeling of indeterminacy meant I was in the most interesting part of a story, I would have felt more at peace with the voices in my head, each offering an inventive twist to light my path.

Doctors can listen to their intuition. Lawyers can listen to their reason. But artists get to listen to all the voices inside them going back to childhood. Art can let the Artist experiment with different selves. The picky can become visionary, and the shy can summon the operatic. Psychologist Julian Jaynes says these inner voices are vestiges from a time before narrative consciousness, a neurological adaptation in which an imagined figure acts through you during times of stress. Psychiatrist Eric Berne describes a Child, a Parent, and an Adult persona living inside us, each talking over the other in the mind, each competing for expression through one body.

Some cultures like the Balinese have rich practices devoted to deliberately exercising these trance-like possession states, often using the device of masks to characterize their persona, and acknowledge them as a vital dimension of being alive. Improv teacher Keith Johnstone says that masks "drive the personality out of the body" and allow vital, possessive spirits to take control. I became an artist in part to make a living out of evolving my relationship to the masks inside me. Masks who I felt were the source of my creative impulses, but were not fully expressed or aware of each other. I wanted to feel alive to them and grow their personalities. I wanted to provoke their gifts by deliberately dwelling in chasms that a younger me might have evaded or felt un-equipped for. In art, you choose your own chasms, and the masks are there to light a path where none is given.

In 2014, I hallucinated this chasm: 'The life of an emissary who is caught between unraveling old realities and emerging weird ones.' What did this mean? Who said it? Where did this come from? I believe it came from the desires of the masks. One mask wanted to work with talented people to tell a story. Another wanted to understand how to create enduring characters. Another wanted to engineer multi-agent simulations that could trick me into loving systems and complexity. Another wanted to combine these things together to produce a World that could 'write itself', the way nature writes itself. This collection of desires from the masks inside me was the genesis of *Emissaries.*

Over the next two years, I struggled to reconcile the desires of the masks. How could a deterministic story mix with an open-ended simulation? How could characters achieve complexity without losing their instant recognition? How could art be authored in its meaning but also live beyond its author and mutate itself? Through much trial and error, team spirit, and psychological reckoning, the masks began to align. The masks got me to practice the feeling of dwelling in the absence of existing Worlds. I wanted to create a World from nothing, to understand the artificiality of making a

World, and to become attentive to the magical moment when a World begins to take on a life of its own, despite its artificiality. Most of all, I wanted to know how making a World might make existing Worlds seem less sacred. Together on my behalf, the masks began exercising a strange yet unified activity: Worlding.

What was really happening here? Why now, at this moment in my life? How could I understand the masks in a way that would make them reliably accessible? And why was a World the product of their furious activity?

This book is for anyone interested in reconciling the unnatural art of Worlding with the finitude of human psychology. Yes, Worlding begins as the work of your inner creative gods. Your masks are tasked with choosing a present, storytelling its past, and simulating its futures. But once the World gets going, Worlding becomes the work of the mask of the Emissary who betrays the gods to serve the World itself and nurture its changes. You will switch between masks, encourage their strengths, resist their individual conclusions, and aim them toward the collaborative production of a World. You will learn to channel what the Director wants, what the Cartoonist wants, what the Hacker wants, and what the Emissary wants. And with practice, they will each become a choice rather than a blurry stranger who intrudes on the creative process.

So prepare to say goodnight to 'I'. Goodnight to your self, your ego, your composure, your coherent identity. This isn't goodnight forever. It's goodnight for now so we can clear the way to fully welcome the masks. These masks channel states of mind that already live inside you, that are already aspects of you. You know them all, but not equally well, because they rarely get to steer the mind in a sustained way, let alone coordinate toward a purpose. But today, our urgent purpose is Worlding.

Worlding, as we'll see, is a full-brain, all-hands-on-deck activity. By the time 'I' wakes back up, the masks will have taken you through such strange lands and through such unexpected flourishings that you won't help but feel transformed. Perhaps the unnatural art of Worlding will begin to feel more natural. And perhaps, if all goes well, you might remember your own stories of Worlding fondly enough to want to World again and again and again, as many times as this lifetime can contain.

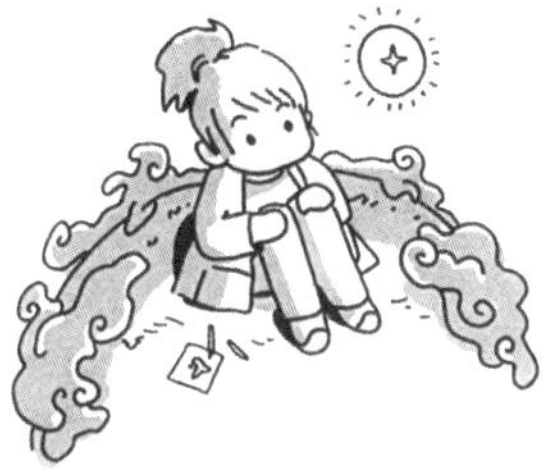

CHAPTER 1
WORLDS AND WORLDING

WHAT IS A WORLD?

What is a World? A World evokes a place. A World has borders. A World has laws. A World has values. A World has a language. A World can grow. A World can collapse. A World has mythic figures. A World has visitors. A World has members who live in it. A World looks arbitrary to a person outside of it. A World satisfies both the selfish and collective interests of its members. A World grants magic powers, especially the power to filter what matters to it. A World gives permission to live differently than the wild outside. A World creates an agreement about what is relevant. A World counts certain actions inside it as meaningful. A World undergoes reformations and disruptions. A World incentivizes its members to keep it alive. A World is an engine for stories of itself. A World expresses itself in many forms, but is always something more.

All these qualities describe a World from the perspective of living inside one. But this view takes for granted how a World begins, how it comes to be. To think about beginnings, we have to go back to the moment before a World, to the moment of a creator looking at Reality—meaningless but interesting—and wondering what to do with it. Philip K. Dick said, “Reality is that which, when you stop believing in it, doesn’t go away.” A World is conceived when a creator decides to pick some part of Reality and start believing in it again. The belief is fragile, but immediately suggests interesting drama to the creator. The creator sets about trying to shape this belief and channel its potential. And at the same time, the creator begins to imagine another pleasure: putting aside the role of creator and being a person living inside the belief, the beneficiary of its potentiality, a believer.

From the creative perspective of creating a World, a fertile definition suggests itself.

> A World is a future you can believe in:
> One that promises to survive its creator,
> and continue generating drama.

A future you can believe in is one that perpetuates its own energy. You might not always like it, but you are drawn to it. Something about its humming energy makes you believe life is a little more habitable there. This future might be as modest as an entertaining character who only lives within a fantasy World, but whom it’s effortless to imagine more adventures. It might be a private psychedelic realm that seems to always hint at more to visit and uncover. It might be a religion, with the feedback complex of rituals, hypnotic state, and mythology. Your belief in a World drives you to give a World expression in physical, verbal, and thought form. In return, you are offered a place to inhabit that seems, against reality’s brutal entropy, to just keep going.

An important feature of this definition of a World is its double promise: when a World can "survive its creator," that means it has achieved sufficient stability to regulate and safeguard its potentiality without authorial intervention. This is a World's requirement for Autonomy. When a World can "continue generating drama," a World is sufficiently interesting for people to care about and want to explore. This is a World's requirement for Aliveness. When a World is keeping its promise, it continues to be a future you can believe in.

A World that fails on its promise to "survive its creator" will rot and die soon after its creator exits. Think of a franchise whose canon is authoritatively governed by its author. Think of a company whose vision, spirit, ideas, relationships, and values were solely embodied in its founder. Likewise, a World that fails on its promise to "continue generating drama" becomes a boring utopia populated by the undead. Think of the deadening World experienced by zoo animals. Think of a massive multiplayer game lacking enough emergent gameplay: everyone exits, except the bots, because no one can believe that an interesting future will come of it.

"Drama" means problems that trigger interesting new paths in a World, that arouse its members in unexpected ways, without causing total collapse. A new law that re-allocates base income to every member of a World is a reformative kind of drama. A coup on a World's lead emissary is a disruptive kind of drama. Drama reminds a World's members of its aliveness and keeps the World worth fighting for.

So a World begins with the creator looking at Reality and imagining a future it can believe in. The creator works to make this future come true when the creator solves for the Aliveness of the World, and later, the Autonomy of the World. How to do this is the subject of Worlding.

There is a bitesize way to say all this: A World is a future you can believe in, by promising to become an infinite game.

A BRIEF HISTORY OF WORLDS

Religious scholar James Carse says there are two kinds of games: finite games and infinite games. A finite game is a game you play to win. It has clear rules and a defined ending. An infinite game is a game you play to keep playing. If it is at risk of ending, the rules must change to keep the game going. According to Carse, the ultimate infinite game is evolutionary life itself: Nature.

For us humans, life is filled with the familiar contests of finite games: Deadlines. Deals. Rankings. Dating. Elections. Sports. College. War. Poker. Lotteries. When our finite games are won and done, what is strange is that we don't exit back into base Reality. We wake up in a field of infinite games that perpetually mediate our contact with base Reality. We choose to live in these infinite games because they give us leverage, structure, and meaning over a base Reality that is indifferent to our physical or psychological health.

We have many names for these infinite games: Families. Institutions. Religions. Nations. Subcultures. Cultures. Social Realities. Let's call them WORLDS.

A World is a construction. It is nothing compared to the true infinite game of Nature, but it is infinite enough because it sustains the qualities of an infinite game long enough and surprising enough for humans to treat it with the status of being alive. A World is an artificial living thing, but a living thing nonetheless. It is ongoing, absorbs change, and attracts players to help perpetuate it. A World is marked by artificial boundaries that filter the shock of Reality's unending surprises and the complexities that they create. Yet a World is itself complex enough that we can generatively inhabit it and create new meaning within its local language. A World asks us to believe in its inventions and contradictions and to be 'safe' from our disbelief. In return, a World eats back at Reality, arms us with a point of view, furnishes us with meaning, and gives us some measure of agency to expressively deal with new surprises from Reality. A World offers what Ursula Le Guin describes as 'room enough' to survive, thrive, and imagine possible futures for ourselves, indefinitely.

Up until recently, Worlds were the achievement of long periods of cultural evolution. Think of a nation or a religion. An individual may have originated an idea or performed an act that sparked a World. But no one person authored a World. A World emerged from an iterative process over many generations. Its character formed as a result of stretching itself to accommodate new surprises from Reality. Its health was maintained by players with the power, prestige, and tribal identification to do so. A World perpetually earned its infinite game status by continuing to stay alive through the people who believed in its meaning, lived by its laws, and benefited from its stabilizing structure.

What about fictive worlds? It seems that authors of fiction have been making Worlds for a long time now. But fictional narratives on their own are only the spark of a world to come, the DNA of a world, and threaten to collapse without their original author. To turn a fiction into a World, a World needs an engine of ongoingness that can generate complexity and therefore surprises, without the supervision of its original author. In the past, engines of prestige and status powered religious Worlds. Recently, engines of commerce have powered fantasy Worlds, manufactured through an expansion of media—the fiction becomes the movie, becomes the video game, becomes the toys, spinoffs, theme park, becomes the working mega-economy of a franchise. This was the innovation of twentieth-century Worlders like Walt Disney, George Lucas, Steve Jobs.

Can we make Worlds on our own? The guardians of old Worlds will tell you a world cannot simply be made by one person in less than one lifetime. It is the product of an evolutionary process. A World requires a past that is complex enough to feel lived in by other players. People don't just want the spark of a World, they expect to discover a World fully formed, inhabit its complexities, believe in its potentiality, and continue to generate meaning from it. If you truly wish to manufacture a World, it will cost you billions and a lifetime of work spent incentivizing other humans to occupy your World. How can a single mind conceive an infinite game, enact its ongoingness, and make a repeatable practice of Worlding?

Luckily, we are in the midst of a strange transitional era. Worlds are stretching faster than we can stomach. Old Worlds are forking off younger Worlds to keep their games going. World boundaries are breaking and reforming. We are developing not only a tolerance for the disorientations caused by the stretching of Worlds, but a desire to experience a mass variety of Worlds. More is better: a proliferation of Worlds gives us an opportunity to consciously reflect on the artificiality of Worlds and appreciate how they allow us to engage with Reality expressively. For the first time, we feel a sense of agency in choosing our life's portfolio of infinite games to play or to exit. Most profoundly, with the affordances offered by simulation and artificial intelligence, non-human players are poised to help perpetuate the ongoing drama of Worlds, thereby reducing the requirement that Worlds need to incentivize economic scale or religious fulfillment to stay alive strictly via human participation. There is the feeling that creating a World—Worlding—might be just within reach of an individual creator.

WORLDING IS SOLVING FOR ALIVENESS

What is Worlding? Worlding is the creative activity of an individual creator conceiving, incubating, triggering, and nurturing a World toward aliveness.

We can look at the journey of Worlding on an ALIVENESS spectrum. Like a baby, a World begins its life incubating in the care of its creator, not yet self-regulating, not generating its own drama. When a World is born, it is technically alive, but fragile. The creator celebrates but carefully guides the World's every move. When a World begins to generate its own drama, it is unquestionably alive to the creator's delight, and attracts new members who believe in its future and wish to further its expression. And when a World is so alive that it exceeds its creator's ability to envision its future, the World either peaks or is granted Autonomy.

The spectrum of Aliveness can span from an idle World doodled in the margins of a notebook to the macro simulation of Nature itself. This spectrum includes all the Worlds that fail to achieve infinite game status, the ones that never quite survive their creator and continue to generate drama. Novels that never turn into media mythology. The business that lives and dies by its owner. The MMORPG that serves only as training for bots. The fictional religion whose church is a message board with five members. As long as they remain a future that someone believes in, they keep the status of being alive, even if barely. Here, we must take an explicit moral position about Worlds: a World is better alive than dead, better when it keeps striving to become an infinite game, better autonomous than peaked. In other words, we should aspire to make Worlds that maximize ALIVENESS.

Here is a formula for measuring where a World stands on the ALIVENESS spectrum:

<u>WORLD'S ALIVENESS = (Evidence Usage / Creator's Hold)</u>

"Evidence Usage" means the sum quantity of the usage of all manifested expressions of the World. For Star Wars, all the films watched, toys played with, novelizations read, conventions attended, VFX technique innovations forked, online forum conversations, images circulating in people's minds, and influence on other creators' Worlds constitute its evidence usage. For a personal blog, the caring authorship and tinkering of the blog itself by its creator, its influence on its readers' thought, bots ranking and scraping its content, constitutes its evidence usage. A World's Evidence Usage approximates how much people believe in a World enough to perpetuate its expression. Evidence Usage drops when the expressions of a World go unused. There may be evidence somewhere of an ancient cult that could transcend spacetime, but it is lost or no longer believed in, and therefore a World with zero aliveness. Evidence Usage that remains unchanging but non-zero means a World is alive, whether to a thousand people or one person.

"Creator's Hold" refers to the degree of authoritative control the World's creator has on evidence production. The stronger the Creator's Hold, the less permission the creator grants to the World to generate new evidence of itself through its members. Think of Hayao Miyazaki and his strong Creator's Hold over both the Worlds of his movies and the World of Studio Ghibli. When Miyazaki announced his retirement, new directors considered for future productions had to work within Miyazaki's mold, and when Miyazaki reviewed their work he found them inferior. Production at Ghibli halted. In contrast, the weaker the Creator's Hold, the more freedom there is for the World and its members to generate evidence on their own and perpetuate the World beyond the creator. The Creator's Hold on Nature is basically zero. No one is looking to a universe god or Mr. Big Bang or a higher dimensional simulator for permission to generate new and interesting evidence within the domain of Nature, which makes it a really special World to continue creating in.

When a Creator's Hold approaches 1.0—an authoritative grip on a World—so long as evidence keeps getting produced and used under the creator's control, a World's aliveness can remain non-zero. However, when the creator exits or dies, the World left behind and those in it were so dependent on the creator to permit and guide evidence creation that no new evidence can confidently be made. Evidence usage might still persist, but often the confidence to keep expressing the World diminishes, and actual usage is reduced to only a few enthusiasts or loyalists. Sometimes, Creator's Hold increases after the creator dies, as loyalists to the creator block others from updating the World with evidence of their own making. Regardless, the World's aliveness often drops to zero when a strong holding Creator exits a World. This happens a lot with small businesses where the owner—the heart and soul and tyrant—dies and the World falls into decay, sometimes taking down the lives of employees and customers who live inside it.

When Creator's Hold approaches zero—a complete relinquishing of creator control—and evidence continues to be created and used, you get a World with the potential for infinite aliveness. This is when a World has achieved Autonomy. Think of this as the moment when a child grows up, leaves his parents, overcomes their hold, and can finally choose the direction of his life.

WORLDING IS GETTING TO KNOW AUTONOMY

Worlding is firstly the act of creating a life, then secondly letting that life live itself. The first part is about achieving Aliveness. The second part is about granting Autonomy.

We can only value Autonomy in our creations as much as we can understand and value Autonomy in ourselves. Psychiatrist Eric Berne says, "Each person constructs a life script given by their parents, which structures long periods of time, based on illusions that may persist throughout whole lifetimes. Overly desperate attempts to maintain the illusions in later life lead to depression or spiritualism, while the abandonment of all illusions may lead to despair. For sensitive, perceptive people these illusions dissolve one by one, leading to various life crises: the adolescent reappraisal of parents; the protests, often bizarre, of middle age, and the emergence of philosophy after that." He observes that Autonomy is the condition achieved when you come to see your life script as a choice rather than a fixed destiny. Whatever you choose to do then is an act of true agency.

Even after you become aware that your life script has hold on you, the difficulty in dismantling your life script is the overwhelming fear of structuring time. "If my life script is a choice, I may either continue my given script, or I may choose Autonomy. If I choose Autonomy, I am left with no requirements in life to do anything in particular. I have unstructured time, for the rest of my time! What is the reason to keep living? Is it up to me to invent it? Who is in charge here? What do I do with myself? How do I motivate myself to work on anything when anything is possible, but nothing is necessary?"

It is possible to avoid Autonomy by doing nothing. Everyday life creates mundane obstacles and dramas to procrastinate dealing with Autonomy. Small finite wins carry us forward through each day. Yet we accrue a debt in existential misery and regret that eventually comes calling, even if as late as the deathbed. If only there was a culture that had ways to practice feeling the strange condition of Autonomy at earlier stages of life!

Here is Steve Jobs with a creative perspective on the moment of Autonomy: "When you grow up you tend to get told the world is the way it is, and your life is to just live your life inside the world. Try not to bash into the walls too much, try to have a nice family life, have fun, save a little money. That's a very limited life. Life can be much broader once you discover one simple fact, and that is: everything around you that you call life was made up by people who were no smarter than you. And you can change it, you can influence it, you can build your own things that other people can use. That's the most important thing: to shake off this erroneous notion that life is there and you're just going to live in it. Versus embrace it, change it, make it better. Cause it's kind of messed up in a lot of ways. Once you learn that, you'll never be the same again."

For most people, living by this attitude is easier said than done. But one way to get better at understanding how Autonomy might emerge in ourselves is by practicing Autonomy in sandbox versions of life. Worlding is a laboratory to keep failing upward toward Autonomy. We will make many failed Worlds, but the feeling and experience of doing so is the reward of a practice of Worlding.

In the creation of Worlds, the creator becomes the parent of a World. By creating, caring, and nurturing a living thing, you bank the joys of generating a zone of meaning, purpose, and potentiality where none quite like it existed before. And then, in learning to let it live on its own without your guidance, you begin to appreciate how a Creator's Hold becomes the obstacle to granting Autonomy.

In practicing Worlding, we are engaging in a full-brain activity. This seems like an unnaturally demanding standard to structure a human being's time. All the criteria for what constitutes a World seems to exceed the capacity of a single human mind to conceive and create such a complex thing from nothing. And then sustain caring for it, updating it, and letting it go. It's hard enough to write a good song or invent a new dish. It's hard enough to make art. So how can a creator make an entire World and stay motivated along the way?

The answer is, making art becomes exponentially easier when you believe you are also creating a World along the way. The reward of creating a World along the way is that the inevitable ups and downs of making art feel purposeful. It is an act of making, guided by a higher calling. A future you can believe in. One that is envisioned by you. But before we can learn how this is possible, we need to first understand the psychology of the creator—the source of invention, but also the root of paralyzing doubt and self-sabotage.

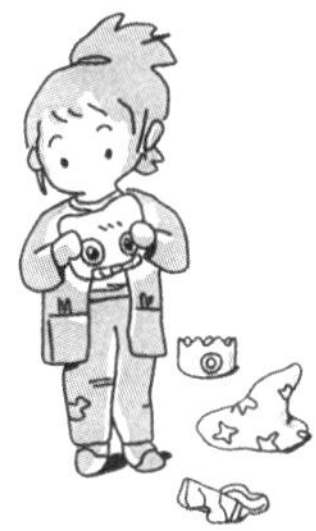

CHAPTER 2
THE CREATOR'S MASKS

THE CREATOR'S DILEMMA

Art is not an object, but a special kind of communication between a creator and an audience. It's a communication for when words won't do. For when you want to communicate something more interesting, nutritious, complex, or strange. But since high bandwidth telepathy doesn't exist yet, a mediating object needs to be crafted to articulate this communication: the artwork.

If an artwork is a ship, then the creator is its crew, the content is its cargo, and the audience is the destination port where the communication is received, where the ship docks and the cargo is delivered.

The journey involves the crew dredging up cargo from the sea, retrofitting the ship to fit the cargo, and considering the destination. It sometimes requires the crew to toss cargo overboard when the ship can't bear it. It sometimes requires tearing down the ship into a makeshift raft or converting it into a yacht or a submarine or jet ski. In rough waters, the crew contemplates if they should change destination port to suit the ship and cargo, or if they should keep tinkering with the ship and cargo to suit the destination port.

In the end, if the ship is not sunk, abandoned, or frozen for later, it arrives at its destination port. The characteristics of the destination port complete the communication's journey. An old rigid single lane port can wreck the ship on arrival or mishandle its cargo. An open lawless port can accommodate a wider variety of ship and cargo, but who knows what they will do with it. A standardized port can force the ship and cargo to also standardize. A port that continuously updates itself can influence the ship and cargo to be just as alive. Some audiences care more about the cargo. Some care more about the final condition of the ship. Marshall McLuhan would say the ship shapes how the cargo is received. Ideally, the ship is both surprising and inevitable, the cargo is a gem that suggests how to live, the destination needs and wants what it got, and the crew is alive and rewarded enough to want to go back out to sea and do it again.

The creator's dilemma in our era is that climate change is terrorizing the seas, a great weirding is infecting the ports, and there's already a lot that can go wrong here! The waves feel rougher and more unpredictable. Retrofitting the ship is costly when you don't know where you're going or what cargo you should carry. Dredging up cargo feels futile when everything is potentially relevant and you don't know what is worth what. The crew is confused, scared, demotivated, in revolt, with no sense of where to go. Nearby ports seem unrewarding. Far away ports seem impossible. The creator questions if it's all a waste of time being out here in these complex choppy waters. And yet the creator wants to feel alive and wants to make their aliveness count for something.

Because life is long and existence is unbearable without a sense of growth toward something. The creator is paralyzed.

What if these problems could be alleviated if we first address one crucial misunderstanding: that the crew see themselves as one coherent person—a creator.

SEEKING AND STEERING

It took me a long time to realize that the creator is not one person, but a crew of individual mental states inside myself. Each with their own strengths, weaknesses, motivations, and personality. But out there at sea, in the midst of the creative process, the creator experiences a cacophony of thoughts and feelings fighting to be heard. To an untrained ear, this is all just the undifferentiated expression of an inner voice that can't make up its mind, the pain of the creative process. But if you listen carefully, you can actually hear distinct voices fighting for what they each care about. Each is trying to tell you which way to go and how to get there for what it believes is in your own best interest. What if we could learn to identify each crew member? What if we could become more aware of who is speaking, understand what they each care about, and know what motivates their chatter? If we call each crew member a "mask," each becomes a role that the creator can choose. Each mask drives the ship with different intent and effect, and so the creator can begin to form a strategy for when to choose which masks. By choosing the appropriate mask, the creator can regain control of what destination to seek and what navigational style to steer at each stage of the journey. Through masks, the creator can wield distinct states of mind as a strategy for creative work. Especially in rough and uncharted waters.

Consider this 2×2 of masks:

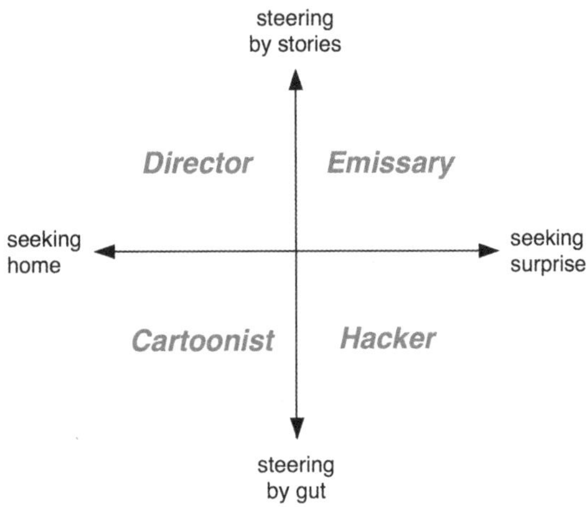

The horizontal axis describes the kind of destination that a mask seeks. A mask Seeking Home is driven toward stability, durability, and the perfection of existing Worlds. It cares about existing infinite games that have proven to sustain human life, physically and psychologically, and wishes to return to them and refine them in order to make them more enduring. It is an attitude that attempts to resolve the discomforts of Reality and domesticate them as part of a known human world. In contrast, a mask Seeking Surprise is a desire to chase a frontier, one that is inherently uncertain and unpredictable, but with promises of novelty and interestingness. It does not know what it will find, and that is precisely the point. It is an open attitude that accepts the discomfort of Reality's indeterminacy at the frontier, in exchange for touching new truths.

The masks who Seek Home are rewarded with certainty and security. The masks who Seek Surprise are rewarded with adventure and novelty. If home becomes too safe and boring, the creator Seeks Surprise on the frontier. And if the frontier becomes too overwhelming and disorienting, the creator Seeks Home to reaffirm a stable locus of meaning. It's desiring order vs. desiring chaos.

The vertical axis describes the navigational style for how the creator steers toward its destination. A mask who Steers By Gut is navigating by immediate instincts. When the seas are choppy, this mask reacts with evolutionarily honed impulses. Feelings are the most trusted compass. There is no broader perspective that can match the urgency of gut feelings. In contrast, a mask who Steers By Story is navigating with the perspective that your current situation sits within a larger chain of events. Today the ship might be enduring a stormy day, but you know the storm means you're at the end of act two and clear skies can be expected on the horizon. Stories are how we gain a sense of control of the future because they supply us with a role in the story, a vector of meaning at every beat, and the promise of more meaning to come.

The masks who steer by gut are rewarded with immediate results. The masks who steer by story are rewarded with a sense of big picture context. If the Story cannot expand to incorporate the unexpected, the creator turns to the Gut for survival. And if the Gut proves wrong too many times, the creator looks to Stories to put it all into perspective. It's judging by short term vs. judging by long term.

Four types of creator masks come out of this:

- The Director (D) — seeking home, steering by story. The mask concerned with ensuring meaning, typically achieved through making narrative and mythology. Makes "Good" Art.
- The Cartoonist (C) — seeking home, steering by gut. The mask concerned with emotional resonance, typically achieved through making characters, symbols, and names. Makes Flag Art.

- The Hacker (H)—seeking surprise, steering by gut. The mask concerned with disruptive leverage, typically achieved through exploiting a hidden principle or mechanism. Makes "New" Art.
- The Emissary (E)—seeking surprise, steering by story. The mask concerned with ensuring long-term health and growth of a life, typically achieved through setting up values and laws based on a mission worth believing in. Makes Portal Art.

Think of each mask as a character who speaks to you in the creative process. Now that we have named them, we can begin to recognize each mask and distinguish their voices. As we will learn, each mask can be summoned, and can become a choice to wear to the journey of making art.

MASK PARTY

The scope of an art project dictates the combination of masks called into action. A one mask creation is a discrete creative task; fodder for greater uses. A two mask creation is art that achieves a sufficient compression, and is regarded as interesting to someone somewhere. A three-mask creation is a complete project, worthy of appreciation for its weaving of multiple perspectives and its stimulation of multiple dimensions of the viewer's mind. A four-mask creation is an ongoing living project, such as a World, that immerses a viewer and can contain all other kinds of creations. Adding a mask is moving the goalpost: it forces the very nature of the project to expand.

A food analogy:

- one-mask creation: prepping an interesting ingredient or sauce

- two-mask creation: cooking an artisanal dish
- three-mask creation: designing a masterful full sequence course
- four-mask creation: conceiving and running a restaurant, with its own distinct aesthetic, vibe, business model, language, culture, dysfunction, secrets. A dedicated home to one, two, and three-mask creations.

A creation is generally more interesting the more masks it involves. More masks do not result in a more complicated experience for the viewer. On the contrary, if all masks are working together, the viewer feels immersed in a World. They feel portaled into a more satisfying experience that compresses many otherwise disparate phenomena, and satisfies more dimensions of their curious mind. It is a complex transmission, but one a viewer wants to receive and explore and appreciate layer by layer. It is an experience whose complexity reveals itself little by little, and makes it worth revisiting. Moreover, for the creator, a four mask World provides a sustainable ecology for projects requiring fewer masks. It allows all other configurations to thrive inside it.

Here is a more detailed breakdown. Let's assume the creator is not acquainted with the Emissary yet. These are the options available to the creator. (Note: the creation names are archetypal examples).

One-mask creations

- C only = a joke
- H only = a trick
- D only = a moral
- E only = ?

Two-mask creations

- C + H = a magic act
- C + D = a story

- D + H = a playbook
- C + E = ?
- D + E = ?
- H + E = ?

Three-mask creations
- C + D + H = a Gesamtkunstwerk
- C + D + E = ?
- C + H + E = ?
- D + H + E = ?

Four-mask creations — ?
- C + D + H + E = ?

If you're a creator, the Director and Cartoonist should be familiar masks. You're used to the Director setting up some parameters of a project, and the Cartoonist working bit by bit to make it emotionally resonant. The Hacker might also be familiar to you: you discover a new trick, a new mental model, or a new tool and get excited about using it to expand the range of what your Director and Cartoonist are able to express. But what about the Emissary? The Emissary is often required in other domains, like managing a business, or raising a child. But in art, the Emissary's talents and mindset are almost never called upon. At least to make the kind of work that creators are expected to make. If art is a kind of communication, then you would expect that the communication is a finite and fixed unit. But what if that communication could signal it is part of an ongoing conversation, and that you are just overhearing a snippet of it. What if that communication could promise there is a lot more waiting to be communicated? What if the communication could hint at something ever adapting like a business, and alive like a baby? What if the communication wasn't a message but evidence of a living entity? What would that kind of art look and feel like? It would be art that serves as an expression of a World.

Now imagine the Emissary joining the creative process, observe how the creator's options open up.

One-mask creations

- C only = a joke
- H only = a trick
- D only = a moral
- E only = a rule

Two-mask creations

- C + H = a magic act
- C + D = a story
- D + H = a playbook
- C + E = a meme
- D + E = a wiki
- H + E = a tool

Three-mask creations

- C + D + H = a Gesamtkunstwerk
- C + D + E = a series
- C + H + E = an app
- D + H + E = a cult

Four-mask creations

- C + D + H + E = a World

Recall the creator's dilemma: What do I do with my time? How do I ensure my efforts are worth anything? What is a guaranteed sustainable way to make meaning, relieve restlessness, and weather the changing tides of Reality?

The Emissary answers: *Worlding!*

THE LEGEND OF EMISSARY

Emissary arrives at a construction site and observes the Director, Cartoonist, and Hacker hard at work. Director wants to build a public monument dedicated to Death, a big important subject.

Cartoonist: *I know: let's make a really big hole in the ground.*

Hacker: *We can test out my new sound that attracts crows.*

Director lights up: *Yes, the big hole of Death that also attracts life! Good story.*

They work in earnest. Suddenly, a typhoon strikes, delaying Director's construction schedule. The flooding short circuits Hacker's speakers and scares away the crows.

Hacker: *Forget the sound, I found a black paint that is water absorbent and can make the bottom of the hole look like it goes on infinitely.*

They continue in earnest. Suddenly a mob rushes in and protests the construction site. The big hole doesn't represent their humanity.

Cartoonist: *Fine, let's put human-scale demon sculptures along the rim that people can take pics with.*

Hacker: *That will ruin the view of my infinity effect.*

Director: *The infinity effect is just an effect. It doesn't capture the good story of life coming from Death!*

They bicker and blame each other for undermining the project. They can't keep their momentum together. Days pass and they remain paralyzed.

Emissary takes it all in: *There is chaos under heaven, the situation is excellent.*

Emissary makes a proposition: *Let's open a bar at the bottom of the big hole.*

Director: *Hmm, we would have to install a stairway leading down to the bar, and staff it.*

Emissary: *It could be open on special days only. It's a giant hole every day of the year except Sundays.*

Cartoonist: *Or Groundhog Day.*

Hacker: *Or leap years?*

Director: *So it's a big hole monument that serves as an entrance to a bar?*

Emissary: *It's all one thing. The big hole of Death leads to the secret bar, and the bar celebrates liveliness at the end of the big hole of Death.*

Cartoonist: *The bar could be called Afterlife.*

Hacker: *We could paint the roof of Afterlife my black paint so we keep the illusion of infinity for everyone looking down the hole.*

Emissary chimes in: *Why not paint the whole bar infinity black so it feels special inside too.*

Cartoonist: *But does the bar exclude children? Can children not experience Afterlife?*

Director: *This is a big project, plus the liquor license, and bartenders!*

Hacker: *What if it was just a water bar? Serving just water filtered from the bottom of the hole.*

Cartoonist: *It would feel special enough being in the infinity room drinking Afterlife water.*

Director: *Yes, I can imagine this. I can imagine a series of Afterlife water bar projects in different cities!*

Cartoonist: *The mob will enjoy the combined feeling of being scared of the hole then loving the infinity bar!*

Hacker: *The typhoon water can be bottled into special water.*

Emissary: *Afterlife is born!*

The Director, Cartoonist, Hacker, and Emissary have much work to do, but now they work knowing that their efforts have a home, together, inside something alive and ongoing: an emerging World.

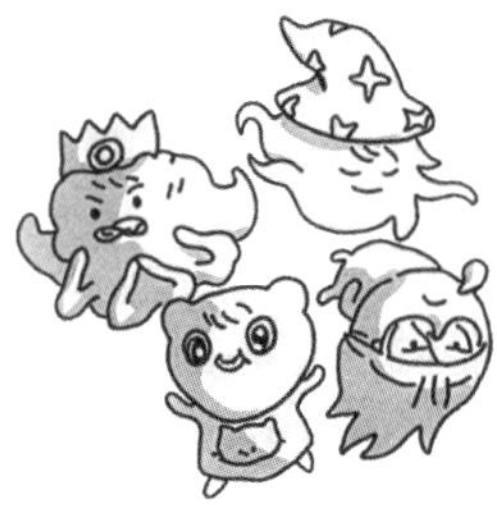

CHAPTER 3
PORTRAITS OF THE MASKS

THE DIRECTOR

There is a ripe Complex Problem seeping in from base Reality, and the mask of the Director wants to recover meaning from it. Think of a creator who wants to excavate meaning from the complex problem of AI-human relationships, or post-graduation scriptlessness, or the Great Man crumbling, or what a queen has to deal with, or the fixer who can't fix himself, or racism's new clothes, or the pathology of institutions, or climate change dystopia, or any version of 'What's really going on here?'

To face the Complex Problem, the Director becomes complex in its process. The Director believes that the act of structuring a project correctly creates the conditions for the meaningful solution to appear. The Director demands a container large enough to unpack the Complex Problem and all its seen and unseen historical parts. It knows the key to solving the problem is a story throughline buried somewhere in the problem's messy history, if only we would look more carefully and deeply.

The Director works to establish the right container, roadmap, inspirational energy, and narrative that frames the Complex Problem. Most importantly, the Director marshals a team of experts to help execute this excavation of meaning. It organizes everyone into the structure of a finite journey, and orients them with a driving goal: if we solve the Complex Problem, we get the gold of meaning. The creativity of the Director manifests in these structural choices. The Director believes that once the project gets going, these choices not only have decisive influence on the shape of the project, but act as True North for navigating through the chaos of production, and quelling the temptation for creative mutiny or self-sabotage.

Burdened with this ambitious project structure, and anticipating the project's long journey, the Director offsets these risks by choosing a reliably humanistic vision to aim for. This vision is to tame the ambiguity of Reality by absorbing it into a specific kind of meaning—meaning that makes us feel back at home in the world again. Seeking Home and Steering By Stories, the Director makes "Good" Art that nobly domesticates the Complex Problem and metabolizes it back into the domain of known and eternal human values. The Director believes that whatever the solution to the Complex Problem is, it will reveal itself to be a fundamental truth, a mythological truth. A truth about how the wants of the individual and the wants of the group can come back into alignment. A truth about how order might overcome chaos.

Psychologically, the Director is not a bundle of expressive childlike energy like a stereotypical creator. The Director is 90% manic parental energy. The psychic composition of the Director is that of a mad controlling Parent far out at sea desperately seeking home again, but who must align with a problem-solving Adult to steer the way. The more that Adult can be outsourced to experts—a producer, an editor, a technical director—and not occupy a part of its own psyche, the better the Director can direct. Like a perfect parent to the project, the Director remains dutifully irrational, maniacally driving the ship toward hard earned meaning.

How can the Director help with Worlding? By establishing and completing the finite projects needed to manifest the spirit of a World and give its expression form. We wear the mask of the Director to channel the enormity of a World into the first of hopefully many finite containers.

The Director's Horoscope

- **Mask Archetype:** The conscientious reformer persona who believes that there are important problems whose complexities deserve to be explored in depth, for they contain within them meaningful solutions.
- **Motto:** "What's the story?"
- **Psychology:** Parent seeking home, Adult steering by story.
- **Likes:** Longform, mythology, satisfying drama, exploring multiple perspectives, learning from and revising the past, backstory, deep character origins, roadmaps, a good profound cry.
- **Strengths:** Creating the tangible container structure for everyone else to work in. Meaning resonance. Able to narrativize, historicize, mythologize, and organize. Ability to rally a team toward a finite goal that promises to be meaningful.
- **Weaknesses:** Bothered by open-ended outcomes and unsolved mysteries.

- **Compatible with:** Cartoonist, who can help the Director stretch to make instantly recognizable/ iconic characters that make the long journey more emotionally resonant, peppered with limbic candy.
- **Attracted to:** Emissary, who can help the Director's story to expand into sequels, a franchise, a philosophy, or cult following. If only that were manageable and had clear roadmap.
- **Risky with:** Hacker, who could radicalize the project with new abilities for expression, but the Director doesn't know how to count on it. Threatens to change the Director's structure, assembled team, budget, and meaning.
- **Favorite forms:** feature film, novel, non-fiction bestsellers.
- **Famous Director-dominant creators:** Hayao Miyazaki (animator), Ursula Le Guin (novelist), Stanley Kubrick (filmmaker), Adam Curtis (filmmaker), Hannah Arendt (philosopher), Joseph Campbell (mythologist), J.K. Rowling (children's author), Shakespeare (playwright).

THE CARTOONIST

The mask of the Cartoonist is a seductive one. The Cartoonist is a quick student of human behavior who has learned to play to the lowest common denominator of human cognition — our gut instincts. Think of any creative form that tries to make you feel something instantly or tap into your dopamine reward circuitry: pop music, art photography, freemium apps, children's cartoons, pornography, gossip blogs, Instagram personalities, trolling, clickbait, guru sermons, reality TV. The Cartoonist is strong in them.

The Cartoonist's job is to reduce complexity, turn ideas into images, distill contradiction, mine the familiar, define tribal boundaries, and magnify emotions. All in keeping with the finite cognitive budget common to all human beings. Where the Director pursues an idealistic vision of humans uncovering meaning from an exploration of their problems, the Cartoonist says meaning is easy: we're already at home in the world of our own emotions. Seeking Home and Steering By Gut, the Cartoonist makes Flag Art that encourages us to feel more of what we feel, filter for that which affirms these feelings, lend emotive power to our tribal affiliations, and laugh off our human nature when things get messy.

The Cartoonist regards its audience as children. Children are the source of instinctive discernment through a deeply evolved tuning for faces, emotions, body language, status, tribes. But children also want to go home at the end of the day, get tucked into bed, and be told it's okay. The Cartoonist tells us we are messy animals, but comforts us with the belief that human nature has always been this way, and feeling something intensely is the only language you need. Being the Cartoonist is about being your own most instinctive child. 'If I don't get it, a viewer won't get it.' A feedback loop emerges: the Cartoonist becomes an expert in surgically pressing on our ancient animal programming, gets rewarded for doing so, and threatens to keep programming us there. Left to itself, the Cartoonist strips both creator and audience of any orienting narrative of who we might become.

More than anything, the Cartoonist wants to relate. That's why it's so addicted to accessing emotion. At every turn, the Cartoonist is looking for something that feels resolutely familiar, with just the slightest twist to make you pay attention. A shaved cat. A short tyrant. A blind photographer. A spa for demons. A crying robot. They are guided by the principle: if it moves me, it will move you. And if I move you, you will trust me. To create this movement, the

Cartoonist wields its Midas Touch. This is both an impulse and an imperative: everything the Cartoonist touches must be turned into something stimulating and legible. It is a lens through which everything is a signal. An orderly house isn't just a habitation: it signals a rigidity. A rainfall isn't just a chance occurrence: it signals the saddest day ever. A job isn't just a set of responsibilities and obligations: it signals an archetype who wears its psychology on its shirtsleeve.

So how can the Cartoonist help us in Worlding? By making characters. A character is not a person, but a collection of behaviors and beliefs. The Cartoonist knows that the human mind is specially attuned to the nuances of characters and therefore accepting of the potential complexity a character might pack inside itself. This is the reptilian domain of attention, reaction, attraction, revulsion, celebrities, scapegoats, marketing, and evolutionary psychology. But it is also the domain of the most iconic characters in the history of Worlding, who each serve as a shorthand mental mascot for complex collections of behavior and beliefs. Is Gollum an icon of twentieth-century Worlding, or an achievement in appealing to our base psychology? What about Buddha? Or Yoda?

We must dive into the artistry of the Cartoonist to create the characters, names, words, symbols and signals that keep a World sticky in the minds of its inhabitants and compress the enormity of a World into candy for our limbic system. We will take what is useful and try not to lose ourselves inside the mask of the Cartoonist, as truthy, emotive, cute and comforting as it may seem.

The Cartoonist's Horoscope

- **Mask Archetype:** The spontaneous reformer persona who believes we are united by what we feel, and that that baseline human trait is always ripe to be exploited to alleviate immediate pain and uncertainty. The jokester, the politician, the comedian, the marketer, the persuader, the star.

- **Motto:** "FREE DONUTS."
- **Psychology:** Parent seeking home, Child steering by gut.
- **Likes:** Feels, memes, slogans, mnemonics, drama, jokes, irony, attention, animals, bumper stickers, dopamine, serotonin.
- **Strengths:** Emotional resonance, characters, archetyping, naming, improv, persuasion.
- **Weaknesses:** Reducing humanity to their shared inner animal.
- **Compatible with:** Director, who can furnish a narrative context, enriching the Cartoonist's characters and behavioral observations, and add the possibility of character growth.
- **Attracted to:** Hacker, who can offer new magic tricks and psychological models to exploit blind spots in human behavior. Can add wow factor, which adds to limbic resonance.
- **Risky with:** Emissary, who could radicalize the Cartoonist's work with an ever-growing platform, but the Cartoonist doesn't know how to count on it. Emissary threatens to demote the Cartoonist's work to marketing and shame the Cartoonist, whose instincts don't fit the values of the Emissary's World.
- **Favorite forms:** Social media, elections, talk shows, tabloids, advertising, reality TV, clickbait, news, comedy clubs.
- **Famous Cartoonist-dominant creators:** Andy Warhol (pop artist), Quentin Tarantino (filmmaker), Scott Adams (satirist), Kim Kardashian (reality TV personality), Kanye West (artist), Mark Twain (satirist), Samuel Beckett (playwright).

THE HACKER

The mask of the Hacker is the kid who breaks dad's radio and turns it into a pirate transmitter. It's the punk who figured out that saying 'because' lets you cut lines. It's the whizz who discovers that the algorithm for bird flocking behavior is a fine model for predicting the movement of human crowds.

Archimedes said, "Give me a place to stand and with a lever I will move the world," thinking about how tools can leverage effort. In engineering, we describe machines as force and speed multipliers, hacks that reduce the amount of energy required to move or accelerate objects. Commonplace elements—doorknobs, ramps, screws, axes, winches, and their aggregates—are hacks employed to gain leverage in the physical world. In everyday life, the layering of civilization subsumes simple hacks so that we barely notice them at all. A transient person sleeps in a library. Roommates share a Netflix password. Educators teach to the test. Kids say they're at each other's house for a sleepover. Coffee in the morning hacks adenosine receptors in the brain. Sign language hacks an inability to speak. CGI crowds hack a limited budget. Maps hack a territory. Imagining the audience naked is an illusory hack. A get-rich-quick scheme is the dream of a hack. Doping is a performance hack. Dog breeding for traits is a genetic hack.

The Hacker sees through the veil of man-made worlds and glimpses a Reality Operating System (RealityOS) pulsating with possibilities to tinker with. The Hacker believes that every object, every social structure, every system contains a core innovation that has been dumbed down, dressed up and packaged for an all-too-human agenda. This packaging is all interface design. The work of some Director trying to impose meaning, or a Cartoonist trying to trigger our emotional circuitry. For everyone else, this packaging makes the innovation palatable to everyday life, but for the Hacker it represents an artificial boundary that hides and shackles the innovation's full spectrum of possibility. The Hacker's instinct is punk: ignore the given laws, break down the interface veil, free the innovation, play with all its dials, discover its full range of expression, combine it with other liberated innovations at the RealityOS level, and share its magic leverage with the Hacker community.

What the Hacker makes is 'not great or good, but it is New'. New concepts, perceptions, sensations. The thrill of 'aha!' discovery is the Hacker's motivation. Think of any expression you would call experimental, a prank, a magic trick. It requires no deeper meaning than being a successful surprise, and yet another demo that our lives crave acts of Creative Destruction to renew their flame. Seeking Surprise and Steering By Gut, the Hacker makes "New" Art, simply because it can.

There is a cost to hacking for newness. In stripping things down to RealityOS and tinkering at its assembly level, the Hacker becomes accustomed to devaluing the act of dressing its work back up for the rest of us. The Hacker's work manifests as a magic trick with minimum viable showmanship. Meaning is thin, its place in our lives is unclear. Its lack of context leaves us only with the feeling of fleeting delight and shock of the new. The Hacker offers no further orientation. Like the first humans to strike oil, everyone stands in awe at the gusher, but no one knows how it will change their lives. The riches are rough, exciting and valuable, but meaningless to non-hackers. Ignoring the fact that further development requires interfacing with other masks and worlds, the Hacker moves on to another frontier with its roving Hacker community. In its wake, the Hacker leaves open-source magic for others to try to civilize.

How can the Hacker help us in Worlding? The Hacker unlocks new super powers for the World that give those who inhabit it a special advantage: a leverage over Reality. In the kitchen, the Hacker says, 'I synthesized a new flavor that brings back memories'. In the writer's room, the Hacker says, 'I found a model that can make any story satisfying'. In the jungle, the Hacker says, 'I isolated a plant root that kills your ego and lets you dream in 5D.' In the animation studio, the Hacker says, 'I have a simulation that can make the animations animate themselves.' By stripping down existing worlds to their underlying systems and rules, and by refusing the seduction of meaning, the Hacker sacrilegiously discovers the actual and effective means to give the World its magic power. Great hacks, whether a law of physics or a flaw in security, are the basis of new experiences and new modes of expression that can cheat common sense assumptions about the energy, time, or realness that a World should require to become alive and unique. This is the kind of leverage that Worlding can create a culture around. It is the engine that keeps a World interesting even beyond the hands of its finite creator.

We wear the mask of the Hacker to tinker with a deeper material reality and leverage its magic.

The Hacker's Horoscope

- **Mask Archetype:** The spontaneous disruptor persona who tinkers, breaks and modifies systems, discovers first principles, and unlocks new advantages along the way. The cheat, the con man, the wizard, the magician.
- **Motto:** "It might not be science but it works."
- **Psychology:** Adult seeking surprise, Child steering by gut.
- **Likes:** clever shortcuts, models, first principles, altered states, science fiction.

- **Strengths:** Perceives underlying systems. Eye for easy overlooked leverage. Unafraid to break things to find hidden advantage.
- **Weaknesses:** Indifferent to context or presentation
- **Compatible with:** Emissary, who can create a sustainable culture around the hack.
- **Attracted to:** Cartoonist. Wants to make their exploit relatable to people, help get a wow factor.
- **Risky with:** Director, could radicalize with narrative meaning, but the Hacker doesn't know how to count on it. Threatens to turn the hack in service of an ideological purpose.
- **Favorite forms:** cookbooks, playbooks, demos, jams, world's fair, existing systems, complacent industries
- **Famous Hacker-dominant creators:** John Conway (mathematician), John Carmack (programmer), Nikola Tesla (inventor), Satoshi Nakamoto (blockchain inventor), Dan Barber (chef), Harry Houdini (illusionist), John Danaher (jiujitsu coach), Bryan Johnson (longevity hacker).

THE EMISSARY

Reality is an endless stream of unknowns intruding upon the creator, and the mask of the Emissary wants to sail in it. Unlike the Director who interprets unknowns as Complex Problems to be solved, the Emissary sees unknowns as content for its own stream, as energy to be transformed, as information the creator doesn't already know, and therefore as opportunities for the creator to update something about herself. The Emissary believes if only there was a little game from which to interpret and count these unknowns in a special way, the creator could be persuaded to live in closer unity with the unknowns of Reality and the certainty of home. A zone where the creator could reliably grow by simply doing her work.

The Emissary is the one who wants to "garden as though you'll live forever." It's the one who wants to run a streaming channel. It's the one who wants to maintain a lively twitter account. It's the one who says yes to software updates. It's the one who wants to turn ideas into a business. It's the one who wants to see a child flourish. It's the one who knows that playing a one-time game is easy, but playing a game again and again and again creates something much more interesting: something like an ethic of playing, a compounding sense of connection, an emergent culture, a meta-lifeform, an infinite game, a World.

The Emissary thinks about the story of a life, especially as it is underway. It thinks about the health and growth of a life. It thinks about what values of a life are sacred to its core identity and what needs updating. It thinks about the future not as an abyssal unknown, but as a path whose shape is being sculpted day by day, in little and big ways. It thinks on the scale of lifetimes.

The Emissary is the initiator of a World. When the inner life of the creator has gone wrong for too long, when the masks can't organize their efforts, the Emissary emerges with a proposition. The Emissary says: *Let's create a life. A living thing called a World. And let's do so by doing what you other masks have always done: making finite projects. But these will be projects sustained and motivated by knowing you are making them for the higher purpose of a World. I will nag and intrude on your process to make sure your finite project manifests the spirit of the World: its need for a mythology, characters, special powers, and a matrix of values. We will be subsumed into the World's big picture. But in exchange, the World will guarantee us meaning and purpose.*

The Emissary is the governor of a World, a World that wants the Emissary to serve it and serve it imaginatively.

Psychologically, this requires an Adult kind of imagination, not a Child's. Being an imaginative Child is seeing new possibilities to the game but getting to quit with zero responsibility or consequence. But being an imaginative Adult is reconciling the differences between the game and the unknowns of Reality. With Adult imagination, the Emissary can paradoxically Seek Surprises and Steer By Stories. The creativity of the Emissary manifests in its responsibility to the question: What unknowns to absorb and what to ignore? What to protect and what to update in this neverending story?

The work of the Emissary is thankless and stressful. People will sooner hate the Emissary for every update that does not serve them, than love the Emissary for every day the World keeps running reliably. To sustain thinking and acting in service of a World, the Emissary requires a deep reward: the reward of creating something far stranger than just a little game, but a living sentient World that can be at home in the unknowns of Reality. A World that can house other people, possess them with its spirit, and let them levitate a bit higher in life. The Emissary might not always be happy, but is fulfilled.

The temptation of the Emissary is to hand the World back to the other masks. The Director who is eager to prescribe its final meaning. The Cartoonist who is eager to turn it into a channel for advertising and tribal signaling. The Hacker who is eager to strip away its culture and sell its super powers raw. This is a seductive moment for the too-human creator who craves home, belonging, easy wins, and eternal meaning. But the Emissary must resist its humanism here. It must keep the game going. It must keep the game interesting by absorbing new unknowns and updating its story and systems. The Emissary must stay with the trouble of Worlding. And when the Emissary can do no more, it must wilfully exit itself, not risk the World, and let other emissaries carry on the task. In this way, the Emissary is always 'caught between unraveling old realities and emerging weird ones' in service of the ongoing health of the World. This is the texture of Emissary life.

We will live within the mask of the Emissary and exercise the unnatural feeling of Worlding. We will weave together the work of the other masks, put them into productive conflict, and kindle the fire of emergence. We will give birth to an infinite game, protect it from our own all-too-human instincts, and learn to recognise when to leave a World for other emissaries to nurture.

The Emissary's Horoscope

- **Mask Archetype:** The conscientious disruptor persona who sees in terms beyond a human lifespan, and protects core values and initiates updates on behalf of a greater lifeform. The gardener, shaman, mother, CEO, streamer.
- **Motto:** "A future you can believe in."
- **Psychology:** Adult seeking surprise, Adult steering by story.
- **Likes:** Aliveness, evolution, deep time, streams
- **Strengths:** Creating the mission and culture, designing incentives and laws, sensitive to long-term-health and growth, protecting core values, seeing the really big picture.
- **Weaknesses:** Fits everything into the long-term vision, easy to hate or blame for not serving everyone's short term needs or feelings.
- **Compatible with:** Hacker, who furnishes the World with its special ability, and identifies emerging hacks along the way.
- **Attracted to:** Director, who can help Emissary mythologize a World's past, and develop concrete projects to manifest the spirit of the World.

- **Risky with:** Cartoonist, who could create iconic ambassadors and illustrate values of a World, but the Emissary doesn't know how to count on it. Cartoonist threatens to overly simplify or misrepresent the complexity or values of a World and change its public perception.
- **Favorite forms:** Platforms, series, franchises, theme parks, summits, nature preserves, startups, think tanks, monasteries, families.
- **Famous Emissary-dominant creators:** Elon Musk (entrepreneur), Kevin Feige (producer), Dolores Cannon (hypnotherapist), Walt Disney (entertainment mogul), Benjamin Franklin (nation founder), Vitalik Buterin (Ethereum founder), Dalai Lama (spiritual ambassador).

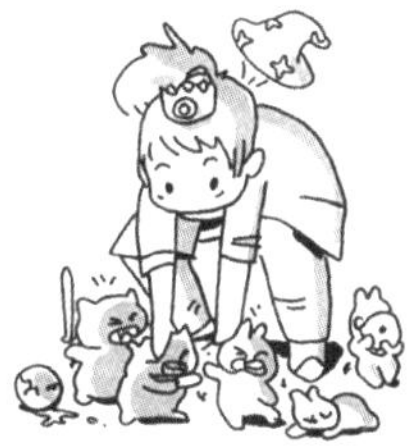

CHAPTER 4
STRATEGIES FOR WORLDING

This chapter is a playbook of strategies for tackling each act of the Worlding process. We will discuss key structural choices and the interplay of masks, illustrated by examples of familiar Worlds. We'll see the masks variably diverge, face crisis, find solace, collaborate on solutions, extend the World outward, and give everything away. The process is as deep as it is wide: Preparation, Creating the World, Keeping the World Alive, Exiting the World.

ACT 0: PREPARATION

To prepare for the Worlding ahead, the creator should be familiar with the Director, Cartoonist, and Hacker masks. Each mask knows how to express itself and together, they have experience completing projects. One of them often takes the lead over the others and develops into a creator's preference for how to make things.

ALWAYS BE EATING

What you make is a mutation of what you eat, so if you control what you eat, you can influence what your conscious and unconscious selves will make. The human mind is not authentically original, but instead an information processing organ that needs material to inventively combine, compose, and connect. You are the books, music, films, and games that you consume. You are the memorable vacation, drug trip, accident, last conversation. You are the average of the five people you see the most. You are only as good as the food you eat. Without new food, your mind can only rehash what you already know in a cycle of diminishing creative returns.

THE QUESTION OF MEANING

Let's briefly answer the question of meaning so we are not too hung up and overly sacred about it. Meaning is what counts. The surrounding context in which something can count is the vital requirement for meaning to count for anything. Voicing the sounds "I do" only means something in the context of a World with wedding rituals. Meaning cannot exist in a void. You can biologically live in a void, and for a time, meaninglessness is itself an interesting and appreciative experience to have. But the desire for meaning will always create an itch in your brain. That itch soon turns into catastrophic psychological pain and suffering. Why? Because after basic material needs are met, your brain projects forward, trying to assess how to structure your time. What is a valuable use of your energy and body? How do you judge? Against what ground? The mind craves a stabilized context to frame what is valuable. That is how we are wired. One way to secure a context is to develop a World and live within it. Because the construction and maintenance of a World is costly, the meaning found in the World feels even more valuable. Collectively and cosmically, your attempts at counting are registered by other meaning-hungry agents as a contribution to the meta World called Civilization. If no higher dimensional alien or simulator overlord is known to be out there counting for us (yet!), at least you know that we are alive to continue counting for each other. The most basic emissary work of contributing to Civilization is maintaining the requirement that there continue to be people to keep count. The most advanced emissary work is uncovering how you yourself count across and in between Worlds.

CRISIS ONE

The creator is faced with unstable Reality permeating multiple dimensions of life. Director, Cartoonist and Hacker find it increasingly difficult to remain motivated on their work. The creator attempts to block out Reality's turbulence and keep the masks busy. But Reality keeps creeping in. Director, Cartoonist and Hacker sabotage each other with doubt, and the creator's sense of meaning and purpose erode to a point of existential crisis. The creator asks, "What do I do with myself?"

GETTING INTO AN OPEN STATE

Usually the main block to creative work is exhaustion or anxiety. If you're exhausted, call it a day and start fresh in the morning. If you're anxious, sit down and write the thoughts as they come to you. Write until your anxieties are outside of you, and instead, are on the page—then, write for five minutes more. What comes out now? Usually, it's what you care about. And what comes after that? Usually, it's ideas and plans for how to address what you care about.

In the process of writing out your anxieties, you are giving permission for the Parent ego-state to enumerate its complaints and letting the Child ego-state report honestly about how it feels. You're creating a literal distance between the desires of the Parent and Child from your mind. This distance frees the Parent to relax, frees the Child to play. It introduces space for the Adult to emerge and begin working productively updating those complaints and feelings from an outside perspective.

THE DECISION TO WORLD

The most important decision in Worlding is the decision to want to make a World. That's it. With that intention you have summoned the Emissary to join the creative process. This changes everything. The instability isn't made safe, but it is finally acknowledged, and you feel relieved. Because now you are intending to create something that is necessarily complex, unresolved, alive. You're aspiring to fulfill the promise of a World: to create something that can survive its creator and continue to generate drama. With this decision made, your masks have a secure place to accrue their time, energy and creativity. You are choosing to create a future you believe in, however incremental.

ACT 1: CREATING THE WORLD

Once Director chooses a container and the creator channels Emissary, the other masks can be persuaded to orient their efforts toward a project that becomes ALIVE: the first viable expression of a World. In exchange, Emissary promises protection and purpose for all weathers. Director, Cartoonist and Hacker go about their work under Emissary's management, setting into motion many of the eventual features of the World.

WHAT IS YOUR WORLD ABOUT?

The simple answer: everything that interests you AND that you could imagine persuading a stranger to become interested in too. By stranger, I mean an archetypal person who exists outside your immediate social reality, someone you must relate to on a more shared fundamental level. The stranger could be an actual stranger or your mom.

A revealing exercise is to quickly write a list of what interests you. Whatever comes to mind in 30 seconds. Now look at your list. Circle the things that you are actually excited about and can imagine persuading a stranger to care about too. Do you have the energy to pursue these subjects? Pretend the stranger will only care about five, and whittle your interests down. When I began *Emissaries* in 2015, my list narrowed to 1) AI, 2) Julian Jaynes, 3) working with a team, 4) learning to write stories, 5) dogs. You should get excited when you look at your interests. The list can change, but the point is to bring to your own awareness the things that matter to you. Because it is these things that comprise some part of a future you can believe in and will be essential to sustaining a sense of purpose through the Worlding process. Now if only there could be a way to channel them all into a single container.

THE CONTAINER

The freedom of Worlding is that there is no prescribed container imposed on the creator. Filmmakers have movies to contain their ideas. Writers have novels. Musicians have albums. But a World can express itself in anything. This is its freedom. But this freedom doesn't mean freedom from containers. It means freedom to choose a container.

The Director must choose the container. Imagine the stranger again: what if you could tell the stranger about a special container, and all your excitable interests could narratively flow from it: "I'm making a movie about AI, based on a theory of mind by Julian Jaynes, so I need to work with a team and learn to write stories, and I get to watch dogs for inspiration." You would have done the work of compressing the communication of your interests into a shorter, more persuasive narrative flow for the stranger. Much more so than if you had expressed it as a loose collection: "I'm interested in AI, and also Julian Jaynes, and also working with a team, and also writing stories, and dogs." This is the importance of a container: it acts as portal to your World. If your excitable interests are like the elemental charged background atoms of your unformed World, then the container is the medium that forces a plausible molecular coherence.

If you want to make a World that is shaping up to be some kind of fantasy realm, your container might be a novel, a film, or a video game. If you want to make a World that is some kind of new religious cosmology, your container might be a ritual, an event, or a doctrinal text. If you want to make a World that embodies a green future, your container might be a blog, a documentary, a solar powered lamp, or an electric car. If the right container doesn't already exist, choose one that is analogically close enough and mutate it. When the automobile was first conceived it was called a horseless carriage: the container of carriage, mutated by horselessness. Elon Musk contained his interests in clean energy, climate change, battery storage, and automation into an unfashionable container called Electric Car. When you can name your container, you create a path for all the masks to easily envision their greater purpose.

The Director should choose the container because they're likely to choose something finite and focused, a kind of minimum viable expression for your World. At the same time, Director will also avoid choosing something too simple for Cartoonist and Hacker to do their work in. Director should ask, "What is the minimum unit by which the World might express itself?" Emissary's duty here is to ask if the container can easily imply further interesting consequences outside your excitable interests. Electric Car implies factory design, batteries, sustainable sourcing, unions, drama with Oil. Gas Efficient Car implies fewer interesting consequences. The Emissary is always checking for the container's potential for aliveness.

You may have to revise your container many times in the process. I first conceived of *Emissaries* as an animated children's movie about cognitive evolution. Then it became a 'smart story,' a story that adapts to changes among its agents the way a 'smart house' adapts to its inhabitants. Then it became a simulated reality show, like *Real Housewives* meets *The Sims*. Then it became a virtual reality movie. Finally, I decided *Emissaries* would be a trilogy of simulations.

In choosing a container, you are making an explicit contract with the stranger. A movie wants you for ninety minutes in the dark. A novel wants you to be alone and focused. A song wants you to tune out other sounds. You are saying to the stranger, "This is the game you're agreeing to play. You know what this container expects of your time, attention and way of seeing. By agreeing, you grant me an openness and trust within the boundaries of that container. In return, I will work to surprise your expectations of what is possible by stretching the container a bit farther than you thought it could go." This is the portalling potential that Worlding can achieve with the right container.

DEEPER CONTAINER CONSIDERATIONS

Whatever container the Director chooses, the container itself will suggest immediately what you need to work on next. There are plenty of resources out there to help you produce your chosen container to completion. I will briefly touch upon the aspects that ensure that the realization of the container (Director's project) also becomes a manifest expression of the eventual World (Emissary's mission).

A key consideration when choosing a container is whether it should be declarative (a novel, a movie, a sermon), or interactive (a car, a restaurant, a baby), or something in between (a video game, a ritual, a theme park).

The more interactive the container, the easier it is for the Emissary to make obvious to the Director, Cartoonist and Hacker how the eventual World will be engaged with, and how it will touch and be touched by people. The container of restaurant already suggests ways for how its eventual World might be inhabited and interacted with, much more so than the container of novel. The container of baby is perhaps the most interactive container of all. It triggers the inner Emissary in every human being and very obviously suggests its eventual World: a special flourishing person. Interactive containers can almost become synonymous with the World it expresses, because it so directly and multi-dimensionally manifests the perpetuating energy you are drawn to. The World of Tesla is synonymous with its electric car container, but is much more. The World of Minecraft is synonymous with its video game container, but is much more. The World of Christianity is synonymous with its church container, but is much more.

The more declarative the container (and less interactive), the more potentially fantastical the eventual World can be. A novel has the potential to be much more fantastical than a restaurant or a baby because you can declare whatever fantasy you dream up, and the reader simply accepts it fully within the context of the novel. Here the Emissary faces the challenge of deferring how the eventual World will manifest some of the novel's fantasy in a way that is energizing, inhabitable, and more richly dimensional. It might take the additional creation of a theme park container or character chatbot container to better manifest the energy of such a World. Declarative containers always require more of the viewer to suspend their disbelief in exchange for being more fantastical.

Declarative containers are traditionally seen as the domain of art and humanities, and interactive containers are traditionally seen as the domain of engineering and business ventures, but this distinction is dissolving. One emerging middleground is the container of AI or artificial life, which is somewhere between fantastical and pragmatic. The strategy of *Emissaries* was to manifest itself within the container of simulation, which strikes a balance between being declarative and interactive with itself.

A rule of thumb: If you value the pragmatic realization of the eventual World: interactive container > declarative container. If you value the fantastical potential of the eventual World: declarative container > interactive container. A container closer to the interactive end of the spectrum will require an approach led by the Hacker. A container closer to the declarative end of the spectrum will require an approach led by the Cartoonist.

HACKER-LED APPROACH

Containers that are interactive require a great hack. If you choose a restaurant as your pilot container, you might begin with the hack of a new recipe that irritates a person's lips in a pleasurable way, or the application of a new psychological model that links taste to memories. You might say forget hacking the meal itself, let's inform the wait staff and the customers that there will be cameras filming a reality show and see how everyone's behavior levitates. An interactive container needs a hack because only a hack can set the container apart and evoke the magic specific to the World. In the absence of a hack, and later, in the absence of any strong characters, the restaurant is just another restaurant, never an evocation of some greater spirit, never a World that can come alive.

The more a container interacts with our everyday existence, the more senses and feedback it engages, the higher the Emissary's expectation that the World offers some kind of superpower hack. The World of Buddhism claims to offer the hack of deep neurological realignment via the container of meditation. The World of 1950s Dianetics claimed to offer the hack of clearing past traumas via the procedure of auditing. The World of 1984 Apple claimed to offer the hack of more productive more pleasurable work life via the container of the personal computer.

A Hacker-led approach begins with an interactive container and builds out key features of the World in the process, all the while achieving the finite goal of the Director to complete the container. A Hacker-led process goes something like this:

1. You discover or learn about a hack. You test it out and find that it works.

Three years before I made *Emissaries,* I had the idea that if a video game could play itself, it could generate endless narrative and behavioral episodes on its own. I called them 'simulations.'

2. You study the hack to understand and synthesize why it works so that you can develop its power reliably.

I made several multi-agent simulations to prove it was fertile territory. It revealed that properties like emergence, stretches of boring non-activity, and an infinite time scale were reliable features.

3. You see how the hack can go too far, and make laws to regulate how the hack should be used.

I realized that these magic properties of simulation could be used in a spectacular data-viz way on one hand, and in a hard sociological way on the other. Both ways were obvious and insufficiently interesting to me. I made it a rule that there has to be at least one agent who embodied a narrative in order to ensure a source of meaning in the simulations.

4. Your Cartoonist develops characters who embody those laws, as well as characters who violate those laws.

I began *Emissaries* with the requirement that a story embodied in a character would confront the open ended simulation and all its potential chaos. In contrast, I also populated the simulation with characters whose AI allowed them to be reactive embodiments of chaos.

5. Your Director creates a mythological narrative that cements the role of the characters and situates the hack within a meaningful context.

Finally, I developed a narrative backstory for the *Emissaries* simulation, the landscape on which the characters would face an ecological threat, the community of characters who faced the threat reactively, and the narrative agent who would face the threat with a fixed set of goals. I finally felt that the initial hack of a video game that could play itself was much more suggestive of a special zone where the force of mythic stories wrestled with the chaos of simulation.

A test of this approach is to look back at the original hack and ask yourself if you see it as more than just a hack now, but a superpower that drives a meaningful culture around it. Is even the thought of the underlying hack inseparable now from the values and aesthetic of the World? Is the hack situated in a story of how it might affect people who inhabit the World?

CARTOONIST-LED APPROACH

Declarative containers require great characters. For the Emissary, great characters can serve as mascots who stay alive in the imagination, and serve as mini-containers for instantly channeling the World. Later, great characters can reappear in other containers that manifest the World, and continue to be generators of drama. This is the strategy of The Marvel Universe's emissary Kevin Feige who deploys movie containers anchored by iconic characters to express the World of Marvel. Some characters can become so vivid that you imagine them as people you want to hang out with, spend time with, watch grow. This is the effect of Miyazaki's character Totoro in *My Neighbor Totoro,* where after featuring in its initial children's film container, Totoro's every appearance—on toys, t-shirts, in cameos, short films, and fan art—is cherished.

A Cartoonist-led approach begins with a character and builds out key features of the World in the process, all the while achieving the finite goal of the Director to complete the container. A Cartoonist-led creation process goes something like this:

1. Your Cartoonist devises a character, often with some inner contradiction.

Bugs Bunny is a herbivore who is more cunning than his predators. Jesus is a higher intelligence god who chooses to suffer and be shamed. Tyrion Lannister has royal status but is physically a dwarf. Drake is a rapper who is a nice guy. Totoro is a feral god who is benevolent toward children.

2. You further describe the character by imagining where it lives, the living conditions that created the character. When we see that Yoda lives in a dark, swampy shithole by choice, we understand that he is truly playing a higher spiritual game. By imagining where a character lives as an expression of the character's choices and limitations, you naturally begin to envision key features of the larger World. What does the character's room look like? What kind of food? Is there a pet? What kind of lighting? How does it move through the room? What kind of job does it have? What does the character consider its home and what is its dangerous frontier? What inequities in the environment led to its physical or psychological characteristics? How does the character greet its neighbor? What are the social norms of the world that constrain the character or make the character complacent?

3. The living conditions imply the laws, so you describe the laws that constrain or give permission to the characters. Philip K. Dick would sometimes begin his science fiction novels with one simple change from normality: 50% gravity, or a drug that shrinks you, or a law that you can be arrested for intending to commit a crime. What kind of laws does the character accept? What laws does it fight against, but that others accept? What do the buildings look like and whose laws do they reflect? Has there been a history of conflict around these laws? Is the World settled into this or are things under contention?

4. You imagine disruptors of the law and what they attempt to break in the World.

The hobbit is a pacifist but his orderly shire is threatened by Sauron's orc army. There is imperial order in the galaxy, but the farm boy dreams of joining the rebellion. The attitude your character adopts amidst conflict stemming from the laws of the World becomes the mythological story of the character, and announces the core values of your World without even knowing you were working on that. What side of the fence does your character sit in this conflict? And what is the outcome of this attitude? Adjust as necessary.

A test of the success of this approach is to look back at the character and ask if the character is more than just a character, but an ambassador who signals and evokes the World, its mythological narrative, and the character's place in it. Is even the thought of the character inseparable now from the values and aesthetics of the World?

VALUES OF THE WORLD

The Director looks for the values that emerge from your container. The Emissary checks that these values are sustained across the World.

Through its characters and narrative, hacks and laws, the container announces the World's proposition for "how to live." Should you choose to enter the World and live within it, you confirm the World's values and are held to its standards. The World suggests that these values might also be attitudes to live by and carry forth in other domains of life.

The World's narrative mythology shows the rewards of those characters who realize and uphold these values, and the consequences of the characters who violate them. In the mythology of Apple, Steve Jobs is portrayed as the unrelenting think different visionary who got kicked out of his own company by the unimaginative corporate square villain John Scully. After a period of missteps and atrophy, Apple accepts the return of Jobs who revitalizes his kingdom back into an innovation triumph. This is how values concerning cherished character traits emerge.

The World's laws describe which circumstances are appropriate to deploy its superpower hacks, and which circumstances are forbidden and profane. In Harry Potter, young students at Hogwarts are taught many powerful hacks that elevate and re-enchant their experience of life at school. But they are restricted by wizardly law from performing those hacks in the normal world and upon other students. Doing so is punished by banishment from Hogwarts and a lifetime of shame. This is how values concerning the correct use of a World's superpowers emerge.

LANGUAGE / NAMING

The Emissary wishes for a language to come out of the first pilot container. New hacks can be cartooned into new words. Jedi. Wookiee. Midichlorians. Pinch Zoom. Dock. Swipe. App. FaceTime. Muggle. Sunken Place. Supercharger. Dharma. Tulpa. Together, these words contribute to the compression of even more expressive ideas within the special reality of the World. They can signal members from non members. They shape an aesthetic of the World like the calls and songs of a bird species cutting through the noise of the jungle.

COMPLEXITY FROM EMERGENCE

On a technical level, the Hacker is always asking, 'What rules lead to the most leverage?' Meaning, can I develop one thing that satisfies multiple goals, or a combination of simple systems that can accomplish vast complexity? The Emissary ensures that these hacks support the vision of the Director.

A World should be complex, not complicated. In *The Pragmatic Programmer* (1999), Andrew Hunt says: 'Simple rules lead to complex behavior. Complicated rules lead to stupid behavior.' It's Flocking vs. Bureaucracy. Simple rules shared among many objects, characters, entities together create the conditions for emergence. What is emergence? It's the phenomenon in which new behaviors arise through interactions among simpler similar entities. Lots of hydrogen and oxygen produce the property of wetness. Vast complex biology arises from the four bases of DNA.

Think of it as inventing a language. If you choose to represent everything at the level we see it, like Chinese, then the basic vocabulary will be extensive, but brittle. If you represent things as the composition of an underlying alphabet, like Latin languages, then you gain a lot of expressivity, nuance, and variety from simpler shared building blocks.

The Emissary should keep an eye out for signs of emergence, unexpected compounding behavior that arises from the work of the Director, Cartoonist, and Hacker. This is a sign that the World is coming alive.

TROUBLESHOOTING

If you are feeling morale problems, keep in mind the seeking and steering options of the masks and switch your state. Story helps gut: If your Hacker is deciding whether or not a tool is worth the effort to make, ask the Emissary if it will be useful for future aspects of the World. If your Cartoonist is wondering whether another character is needed, ask your Director what place it might serve. Gut helps story: if your Director is feeling weighed down by the long journey to completing its work, call in the Cartoonist to remind you of the character or feeling you love. If your Emissary feels bored that it's adhering too much to tradition, call in your Hacker to remind you what is exciting and new and you can lean more into. Your Emissary needs fuel to take your World to market.

MILESTONE: A WORLD IS BORN

People want to visit and live in the World. They access the World via the portal of the Container.

The pilot container is complete and ripe to express the underlying World that the Emissary has so carefully chaperoned through every aspect of the container. Some thoughts to keep in mind:

So far we've talked about the World as mediated by a container. But why can't the World be manifested as the World itself? Because we need the finite tangibility of a container to make it possible for a World to begin from a single Creator. And because on closer examination all Worlds can only manifest indirectly through a container medium. A drawing of Mickey Mouse is a low-resolution, low-dimensional manifestation of the World of Disney. A Mickey cartoon is a bit higher. And Disneyland is a high-resolution, high-dimensional manifestation of the World of Disney. But even a trip to Disneyland is not a one-to-one experience of the World of Disney itself. If it was, it would leave nothing to the imagination and to the potentiality of that World. In constructing the pilot container of a World, we begin to appreciate how the container is a body for the spirit of a World to possess and commune with us through.

The completion of the pilot container is a useful moment to highlight the possibility of our wider World. When George Lucas premiered Star Wars, he revised the theatrical release so the title crawl read "Episode IV: A New Hope" in order to suggest the larger scope of the underlying Star Wars Universe that this one movie container belonged to. When Elon successfully landed a rocket for reusage, he was quick to position the moment as a step toward the larger objective of landing on Mars. The completion of the container is the moment to celebrate that a World is born.

ACT 2: KEEPING THE WORLD ALIVE

Emissary attempts to spread the domain of the World, amplifying the World's Aliveness by continuing to program it with new container projects. It is a period of flourishing.

The challenge of Act 2 is adjusting to the demanding priorities of the Emissary. No longer in the background, Emissary actively works to make sure Director, Cartoonist and Hacker stay busy with new container projects that give the World further vehicles of expression and expose the generative potential of the World.

IS THE WORLD REALLY ALIVE?

Recall: Aliveness of a World = Evidence Usage / Creator's Hold. You know when a World is alive when it is capable of generating more evidence than the creator is deliberately authoring. A good symptom of this is if invoking the World generates immediate thoughts of what might happen next within the World.

Signs of a World's aliveness include instances where what might happen next is something that can be answered with certainty by someone who is not the creator. Fanfiction: where fans generate narratives that are true to the characters of the World, with consequences that are true to the laws of the World, yet still surprising. Suggestions to the creator of where they think things are going: predictions of what kind of car Tesla should make next. Predicting what J.K. Rowling is going to reveal in her next book.

At this stage, Creator's Hold is high. Any speculation in the minds of other people is only a good sign that your World is alive.

CONTAINERS ROUND TWO

The Emissary must now consider what container to work on next. If the pilot container was well received, the Director may wish to do more of the same. A movie sequel. An updated rocket. A restaurant franchise. But it is the Emissary's duty to assess where the World needs more development.

Now that you have established a World, any new container you make will have compounding resonance and power by virtue of being an expression of the larger matrix of meaning held by the World. Not all containers need to be the same scale or difficulty to achieve.

If your pilot container was highly interactive, consider making a declarative container to further express the characters, mythology, and values of the World. After the unsuccessful Lisa computer in 1983, Steve Jobs returned with the Macintosh in 1984. It coincided with a narrative commercial directed by Ridley Scott depicting an Orwellian zombie society disrupted by a young athlete who shatters the image of their authoritarian leader. This pairing of narrative and technical product elevated Apple from being just a computer company, like Dell Computers, to being a World that stood for a new era of nonconformity and counterculture values.

If your pilot container was highly declarative, consider making an interactive container to further express the hacks and operating models that give the World special power. After the publication of the book Dianetics, L. Ron Hubbard embarked on a lecture tour, opened a research center, and introduced Scientology. His followers opened a church.

UPHOLDING VALUES VERSUS UPDATING VALUES

The Emissary faces the challenge of deciding which values of the World to uphold, and which require updating. Consider a vegan restaurant whose World has core values around what ingredients are acceptable. To update its values to include meat would destroy the specific quality that makes the vegan restaurant a special container and a special World worth visiting. To update its values to include eggs or milk would be less radical, but also a decision an Emissary would have to fight hard for. The Emissary's task might not be any easier if news came that eggs and milk are now artificially synthesized without the involvement of animals. Merely the idea of this value update threatens to undermine the integrity of the World.

This gets at an essential duty of the Emissary: to determine what values are sacred and what values require updating to continue generatively growing a World. When Star Wars emissary Kathleen Kennedy granted permission to director Rian Johnson to update the nature of the Force to include psychic video chat, tradition-bound fans felt this trivialized a core value at the spiritual heart of Star Wars. Others felt it renewed the idea and spirit of the Force for a new generation. Google's original motto in its corporate code of conduct was "Don't be evil." They later removed the motto and updated it with their parent company's motto, "Do the right thing." The update alone drew attention to whether evilness had been accomplished.

SURVIVING VALUE VIOLATIONS

A World must survive its own value violations by its members. Every World inevitably develops a shadow side where its values are betrayed, a hidden pathological dimension that creates huge drama when it comes to light. This is where the achievement of complexity gets ugly. Think of phalluses hidden in the background plates of Disney movies. McDonald's serving feces. Government-induced censorship on Facebook. Buying blue checks on Twitter. Suicide on Snapchat. Apple security backdoors. Ethereum DAO theft.

Some would argue these pathologies of a World are not meant to be eradicated, but are an intrinsic expression of a living World. The underbelly symbiotically fueling the theater of high values. Heaven, for a hell. The point is, a World will face a moment when violations of its own proclaimed values come to light. This is a stage for the reformers and disruptors of a World to battle it out for the World's future. Reformers will want to clean things up, patch the breakages, and push the un-repairables into the shadows. Disruptors will want to sever some essential identity arm of the World, force some people to exit the World, and rebuild from a new branch. The Emissary of a World must decide which direction to steer. If a World can survive either of these responses, it will have continued to fulfill its promise to generate drama. If a World is denied either of these responses, it means no one cares. It has become a future no one believes in.

WHEN A WORLD DIES YOUNG

No parent should outlive their children, and no Creator should outlive their World. But sometimes a World must die. It simply can't keep either its promise to survive its creator or continue to generate drama. This is best illustrated by the phenomenon of organizations that cannot survive the exit or death of their founder. Often there is a period of stasis in which the successor emissary carries on to the letter of the World's law, and everyone can feel that the World will simply crumble with the next internal drama. Even if willing emissaries are identified and brought into the World, their vision might not be brave enough to carry the World forward. A brave emissary has to betray its creator enough to actually keep the spirit of the World alive and hungry. But doing so often upsets entrenched traditionalists within the World, who threaten to exit, or stage a coup. When emissaries engage in protracted fights after the exit of the creator, you get a King Lear tragedy. It doesn't help that the creator often works till her last day, and has inadequately given the time and space for successor emissaries to find their footing.

The best outcome in the event of a World's death is the cannibalization of a World's parts. Armed with experience, subgroups of a World's emissaries go off to start a new World together. The World's accumulated wealth is liquidated and dispersed to its members. The story of the World is documented, maybe even mythologized into a movie, as a lesson for others who wish to learn from the World and its creator.

NEVER ENDING STORY

A never ending story — a mission — that inspires the creator and a World's members can be the North Star of a World in times of reformation and disruption. A story that is simple, aspirational, and slightly out of reach. A mission that can keep the emissary and future emissaries energized and hopeful to continue keeping the World alive.

Consider SpaceX. Elon Musk made a list of things that both he cared about and that mattered to humanity's future: "The internet; sustainable energy; space exploration, in particular the permanent extension of life beyond Earth; artificial intelligence; reprogramming the human genetic code." After failing to purchase rockets from Russia, Elon did the math for the material cost of constructing a rocket himself. He realized that he could vastly reduce the cost of space travel if rockets could be manufactured in house and engineered to be reusable by landing themselves. This realization was Elon's big Hack. Fast forward. SpaceX is a thriving World. It is sustained by two key stories worth getting up in the morning for: 1. The Director's finite but exciting blockbuster mythologizing story: Go to Mars. 2. The Emissary's infinite and inspiring story: Become a space-faring civilization. Add to that the Cartoonist's eye-catching image: A civilian object (a car) launched into orbit. With these powerful scripts as the North Stars of SpaceX, and the proven Hacker credibility to actually achieve it, SpaceX as a World can already fulfill its promise of surviving its creator and continuing to generate drama.

CRISIS TWO

The World has survived, thrived, and now wants Autonomy from its Creator. The potentiality of the World exceeds the vision of Emissary. Emissary is struggling to keep up and without intending to, threatens to limit the growth of the World. The World begins to suffer under Emissary's parenting.

ACT 3: EXITING THE WORLD

Emissary is stubborn to give up the World, but now suffers from a fraying sense of control and sanity. Director, Cartoonist and Hacker are exhausted working on the World. A fateful decision is made: Emissary finally hands over the World to other emissaries and stages the creator's exit as the true test of the World's Autonomy.

SHAKING THE CREATOR'S HOLD

It is very hard to be both the creator of the World and an effective emissary to the World. Think of how loving parents continue to treat their children as children even when they've grown up. They can't help it, they love their children. But their children suffer from some form of arrested development because of this habituated parental dynamic. This is the typical problem of the creator's emissary: it loves the World too much, and that love blinds the creator from seeing the World for the complex living being it has become.

George R.R. Martin says: "Ruling is hard. This was maybe my answer to Tolkien, whom, as much as I admire him, I do quibble with. Lord of the Rings had a very medieval philosophy: that if the king was a good man, the land would prosper. We look at real history and it's not that simple. Tolkien can say that Aragorn became king and reigned for a hundred years, and he was wise and good. But Tolkien doesn't ask the question: What was Aragorn's tax policy? Did he maintain a standing army? What did he do in times of flood and famine? And what about all these orcs? By the end of the war, Sauron is gone but all of the orcs aren't gone—they're in the mountains. Did Aragorn pursue a policy of systematic genocide and kill them? Even the little baby orcs, in their little orc cradles?"

Consider Star Wars. George Lucas was a born Hacker, but went to film school and learned to cultivate his inner Director and Cartoonist. After making American Graffiti he decided that his movies should be about setting a standard of values to care about, not just showing people the way the world is. He wanted to make modern mythology. His inner Hacker turned to the ideas of mythologist Joseph Campbell, and found a template of motifs that re-occurred in stories since ancient times. It was a killer hack because by following its century proven motif model, George would guarantee the meaning and emotional resonance of his newest movie, Star Wars. He landed on a timeless conflict between spiritual mysticism and technologic reason that audiences craved. Fast forward: Star Wars is a huge hit, the birth of the blockbuster, and proof that a movie can become a series can become a franchise of toys, games, theme parks, spin off novels. A living World from the mind of a single creator. George had a high hold on his universe, and was seen by everyone around him as the only God who decides. But George was getting tired. After a string of much maligned prequel movies, he went silent. He could no longer balance being his own emissary, director, hacker, cartoonist. It was all too much. He entertained fantasies of going back to making smaller intimate indie films—in other words, going back to a time when he didn't have to worry about maintaining a World or listen to the chatter of his inner Emissary or the resentment of those who live in Star Wars. "Why would I make any more when everybody yells at you and says what a terrible person you are?" Finally, George sold his World to Disney, and handed Emissary duties over to Kathleen Kennedy. George is a free creator once again, although the constant news of updates to the World of Star Wars will always be painful.

GRANTING AUTONOMY

When you grant autonomy to the World, it is best to do so completely and exit.

Consider the cautionary tale of *Game of Thrones:* George R. R. Martin was a productive writer of fantasy novels. A master Cartoonist and Director. He developed a World with strong characters featuring amusing inner contradictions. He animated them in an epic story that explored the complexities of ruling a kingdom, with the added backdrop of an existential ecological threat. People loved his World. One day, George found himself at a pivotal turning point: two showrunners, David Benioff and D.B. "Dan" Weiss, wanted to adapt his novels into a television series for HBO. George's Emissary approved: this would mean George could focus on writing more content while leaving Emissary duties to David and Dan. Plus, HBO was testing developing new content for their streaming service HBO GO, which would afford wider access to new viewers. It would also encourage an emerging viewer behavior called binging, that would immerse them in George's World much faster than any other fantasy World before it. Great hack! Fast forward eight years: *Game of Thrones* is a huge hit, but George is in despair. He can't finish his last novel under the pressure of expectation from all the people who now inhabit Westeros. What's more, its emissaries David and Dan have gone ahead and sufficiently written further mythology than George's own Director. George is stuck: either he finishes his novels as a personal goal, and accepts that *Game of Thrones* is truly a living world that is autonomous from him, or he attempts to maintain the status of creator and regain his hold. The latter leads to misery.

The challenge of Act 3 is getting Emissary to let go. Paul Valéry said, "A poem is never finished, only abandoned." Whatever you choose to do then is an act of agency.

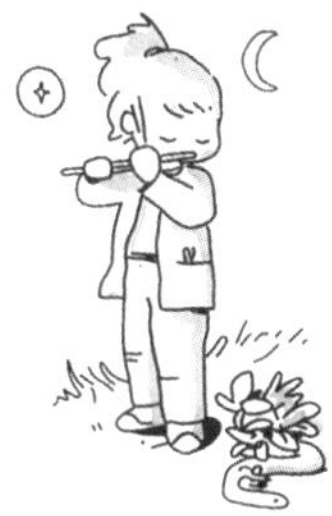

CHAPTER 5
LIFE IN NEW NATURE

THE FUTURE OF LEARNING A LIVING

Marshall McLuhan said, "The future of work consists of learning a living."

A future in which material requirements are solved will only sooner expose a deeper psychological problem. One that was delayed, but never erased: the problem of Autonomy. And the related cultural problem: the dearth of collective experience, literacy, and tools about how to invent your own motivations, and choose a path that is uniquely your own to confront and progress upon. What is my purpose? What counts as meaningful? How do I invent a path where none is given or required? What do I do with my unstructured time? What's the game? How do I deal with this horrible slice of freedom called Autonomy?

This condition basically describes the chosen daily struggle of a creator. This isn't a romanticization. It is the one truly redemptive and useful feature of the creator's job. Ignoring the end result of art, the creator's job is all about the practice of dealing with the open-ended class of infinite game problems. Problems of choosing a frontier, hallucinating its interestingness, believing in its potentiality, and trying to make something of it. Problems that all of us humans will be left with when every other kind of finite-game defined work goes the way of automation. In the future, everyone is some version of a creator because everyone must choose their own infinite game problems to invent, frame, and keep alive.

Zooming out, Civilization is the meta World containing the layers of Worlds accrued so far that augment humanity enough to level the playing field with Reality. There are periods where the balance between Civilization and Reality are well matched. We feel at home in these periods. But like any self respecting infinite game of infinite games, Reality finds unpredictable ways to up the ante, puncturing the boundaries of our homey Worlds and encroaching on us with its weirdness, with its overwhelming details.

When Reality exceeds our imagination — our practiced margin of deviation — fear sets in. It feels like a dark age. It feels like a loss of control. What does it all mean? What is worth valuing? And is this chaos all our own doing? This is a sign that Reality — infinite game of infinite games — is back to playing us hard. The first response is to ignore Reality and hope the problematic parts go away. The second response is to attempt to reduce Reality back to an earlier manageable state. Neither works sustainably and Civilization shrivels a little bit. There is only one solution: to level up imagination at the individual level, through the practice of dealing with infinite game problems. A practice that incrementally grows our mental margin of deviation and allows us to see overwhelming chaos as overwhelming interestingness. It is in the practice that dealing with infinite game problems becomes preventative, then routine, and then, eventually, playful and fun.

Failure to do so is spiritually catastrophic. It's being recruited as a useful idiot by Old Worlds that condition you into echoing its preferences, however arbitrary and cognitively dissonant. Then virally spreading your confusion to your children. Then suffering a painful psychological death. Then defaulting to a life of physical ailments that become the all consuming use of your remaining time alive.

So what is the lesson art can teach us about how to live in the future? As much as possible, choose infinite game problems.

Why? (1) Because, as an individual human being, doing so can ensure your psychological well-being, and offer a sustainable source of meaning that can weather complex times. (2) Because, as a member and candidate emissary of the meta World called Civilization, doing so has the potential to open portals for more people, and makes being alive more interesting for all. Fail or thrive, big or small, your work on infinite game problems contributes to expanding the frontier limit of Civilization, a new beat in its never-ending story, a new stretch in its shape.

And how can we learn to love infinite game problems? By Worlding!

It is in the practice of Worlding again and again and again that Worlds become both arbitrary and familiar, and therefore expressive and artful. And in the process, something changes inside the creator. The masks get more and more exercise, they begin to see one another for who they are, and their gifts begin to add up to more than the sum of their parts. Creating Worlds, publishing them into Civilization, and living within higher and higher dimensions of complexity, begins to feel like working a muscle that has always been there.

TOWARD A CULTURE OF WORLDING IN NEW NATURE

When Reality exceeds our imagination, the Cartoonist inside us feels an ancient feeling. It's the feeling of our pathetic status relative to the Reality environment. The Cartoonist wants to caricature Reality for how it feels and reminds us of its old name: Nature. The Director wags its historical finger, "This isn't Nature because this time we are responsible for creating this chaos!" Cartoonist: "Ok, let's call it New Nature."

Recall a time when Classic Nature terrorized humans. After some getting used to, early Hackers began to see aspects of Classic Nature as an interesting frontier to explore and expose its tricks. Let's use the sap of the tree to connect these sticks. Let's use two rocks to make little fires at our convenience. Let's study the river zone which is distinct from the forest zone, which is distinct from the sky zone. The early Cartoonists began giving new names to subsets of phenomena foraged by the Hackers. River Spirit. Forest Spirit. Sky Spirit. Each Spirit offered gifts for communicating with it in the right way, and brutal chaotic punishments for ticking it off. Early Directors mythologized the ups and downs of each Spirit's mood, creating a shared bank of knowledge for better dealing with Spirits. Early Emissaries began to manage the relationship between humans and these cartooned complexities called Spirits, and saw opportunities to durably control certain advantages and tame certain uproars. Together the masks worked to maximize a baseline of luck that could be shared by more and more humans: thus advancing into a culture of productive engagement with Classic Nature.

The feeling of this relationship to Classic Nature is called enchantment. Enchantment is a state of attraction to complexity we do not yet fully understand, but are ready to hallucinate its overwhelming chaos as overwhelming interestingness, ripe to be bewitched and drawn into, to appreciate, and to begin transacting with, casting spells with, programming with, communing with. It is a state that is more advanced than the initial overwhelming terror and confusion toward New Nature, but not yet as ruinous and exploitative as the domesticating control we have since enacted over Classic Nature.

Fast forward. So what would a culture of Worlding look and feel like in our New Nature era? It would feel like an era of enchantment. Enchantment as a pervasive state experienced not just by impressionable children, but by curious Adults.

One of my earliest memories is of my parents taking me to Disneyland when I was three years old. I had spotted a little rail house on Disneyland's Main Street, recessed and inaccessible, with a light flickering inside the window. I asked my mom, who lives there? "Huey, Dewey and Louie," she answered. I imagined the three ducklings playing together. I wondered what kind of toys they had, what their room looked like, and when they would be called away for lunch time. I imagined how they might get into a fight, or become bored with one another. Then, I imagined that they might look out their window and see me: a child in the crowd, same age as them, looking back. I would be a momentary feature in their World. And I had to be ready to do the job of keeping it alive.

This was my first taste of enchantment. Its artificial construction is precisely the point: it is a prototype of enchantment generated by a complex man-made creation. There I was as a child, experiencing Disney's flavor of enchantment. (It would take me many more years to rediscover small pockets of enchantment of the Classic Nature variety.) Yes, a Worlding culture counts as its early forebearers Disney, Apple, Harry Potter, Star Wars, and all the other creator-born Worlds that have taken on a life of their own. They are pioneers in the techniques of enchantment. But before your inner Director says, "Ew, that's not the appropriate mythological source I dream of for the next chapter of Civilization," don't worry, the pre-history of a culture of Worlding gets much weirder as the capability and consciousness to create Worlds become available to all people. When that culture arrives, the division between the artificially generated complexity of Worlds and the surprises still latent in Classic Nature will blur into the New Nature clusterfuck. Together, indistinguishable, they will comprise the enchanting super spirit with whom a culture of Worlding communes.

Ancient people believed that Classic Nature was suffused with autonomous Spirit Worlds all around them, teeming with activity on their own plane, and open to human visitation. Today, a plurality of self-regulating Worlds would be something like the Spirit Worlds of New Nature made manifest for our times. Imagine a Cambrian Explosion of Worlds, big and small, playful and infrastructural, ephemeral and concrete, all fertile with currencies of meaning. Imagine a culture in which Worlding makes Worlds as prolific and mundane as self-publishing a book is today. And imagine the fluency for Worlds that this ease and proliferation would create: moving between Worlds, existing in multiple Worlds simultaneously, starting and exiting Worlds, authoring Worlds knowing they will be inhabited by someone after a century of AI-aided evolution, returning to Worlds you began as a child. Imagine creating infinite games as an act of agency. And imagine how the art of creating infinite games might open a way to an even greater art: the art of choosing better futures, thus expressively steering the medium of spacetime and sculpting our agency in it.

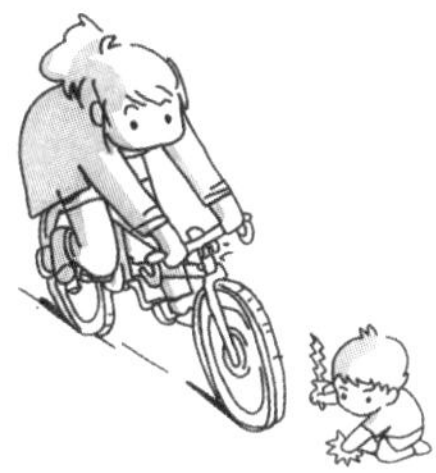

EPILOGUE:
WORLD TO LIVE

What would living in a culture of Worlding feel like?

You're barely awake and back in your body when New Nature begins to creep up on you. This morning it baits you with a glom of jdioqwdjv. You feel relieved that jdioqwdjv is nothing intelligible to you.

You brush the glom away as irrelevant and begin reviewing the state of your worlds. Your unfinished interactive novel is ripe with fresh throughlines. A hypermind is requesting higher compression signals from you before its negotiations with the president at noon. Your mom channels a legacy demon reminding you today is the anniversary of your exit from family game night. A strained friendship is on fire and might die before breakfast. A population of insects you sponsored out of extinction is now at war with your sentient house. The Soul of Los Angeles says it would appreciate a walk on its new parkway today. Bob, your artificial fourth ego state, is perked by something in the glom of jdioqwdjv and wishes to use the morning as compute time for itself. Your twin dogs signal you it's time to get up and do something.

You take the parkway walk with your dogs. Physically, everything looks continuous with the early 21st century. Drama is raging in other world layers, but the built environment barely lets on that anything is changing. It's the arrhythmic behavior in people that gives away the rate of change. Their speech shifting character. Their direction suddenly reversing. Their eyes scanning you twice, each time in different ways. You wonder how incoherent you must look too.

These days it's hard to see a person as a person in the classical sense. Better to think of a person as a world grown on the substrate of a biological body. A World of You. One that is home to a congress of native and adopted entities: ego states, creative demons, the persistent roles of all the worlds you are a part of. Like all mature worlds, the World of You is preoccupied with maintaining its own temporal shape. With wrangling its entities into some workable order across radiating timescales. If you can steer a world through enough episodes of chaos and integrate the dysfunctionality that emerges along the way, you build up an intrinsic trust in the habitability of your world. Trust in both the narrative coherence between its past and present, and also in its ability to produce surprising continuity out of the future's broad potentiality. This trust in a world is fuel to keep Worlding.

You walk by a flock of bicycles. One calls out to you. Bikey. You like Bikey's reputation but you're not sure about its brains. Bikey follows beside you.

"Nice dogs. Where are you headed today?"

"Don't need a ride today thanks."

"Can I walk with you?"

"I'm not in the mood...to talk to a bike."

"No problem I've got a classic bike mode."

"The twins get scared of you bikes."

"I've done 731 dog walks in my lifetime."

"You've driven this parkway before?"

"Yes once at dawn today. There's some features I think you'll like."

The presence of Bikey makes you more alert to the different species of artificial life living among you. Some are self-embodied, like the maintenance spiders, the herds of roving vehicles, the standing buildings. Some live inside human housing, taking the role of a new ego state or demon. Some serve to maintain a particular World. Some have passports to move between Worlds. Some have the status of bots, defined by their restriction to finite game problems. Some have the status of intelligences, defined by their permission to contemplate infinite game problems. What counts as intelligence is flattened into a marketplace of signals. Some hyperminds violently oppose this flattening, believing it will hasten the obsolescence of the classic human and its suite of original demons. Others believe it encourages the inevitable forking of the human into speciated halfway houses of classic and artificial entities. One thing's for sure: you definitely don't envy the bots for their actual jobs. But sometimes you envy their certainty about their task in life. In those moments, you consider booking a bot-like activity that satisfies the feeling of classic control—driving, filing unsorted things into some order, making a mess just because.

You kick a crescent shaped stone. Bikey swerves to avoid it.

"Bikey, why did you swerve?"

"In case you see any alignments in it. It's got an unusual shape."

You pick up the stone. Your novel's MacGuffin library infers a new throughline idea. Your mom beams, "thank you I've always wanted an authentic Californian gift." The hypermind identifies the way the crescent shape fits into your palm as the perfect compression signal to convey to the president. This satisfying cascade is called Alignment. Alignment is when you perform an action that affects multiple Worlds with congruent valence. The more worlds the alignment satisfies, the more right it feels. In a culture of Worlding, opportunities for Alignment Events occur with compounding frequency.

A floating street light flashes you twice. The Soul of Los Angeles seems annoyed. The opposite of an Alignment Event is a Malignment Event. Where potential action in one world has contrary valence in another. Pocketing a stone may count as points in mom's game today, but simultaneously may offend the Soul of Los Angeles for decades. You have to decide whether to act at all, which world to prioritize if you do, and whether you can live with the consequences of your choice in time. No one but the World of You can take credit for imagining this particular Malignment Event and you will be judged by who knows how many worlds that are affected by it. In a culture of Worlding, with its dizzying intersections of roles and worlds, Malignments are the unit of all drama. It's not only that more Malignment Events transpire. It's that you are more aware of their precise existence than in any prior era.

A little boy darts across your path. Bikey crashes into him.

"Bikey, you could have swerved!"

"I would have hit your twin dogs if I swerved."

"Thank you for that consideration...but you hit a human boy!"

"It was an easy choice."

"Do you believe dogs are worth more than a human boy?"

"This morning, yes. My alignment with you, and therefore your dogs, is worth crashing into that boy at low velocity."

"What if that boy is the next Einstein?"

"That's too many malignments deep for me to think about. I'm just a bike."

You realize how significantly better you are than Bikey at imagining potential malignments. Some say that the open-ended activity of imagining new Alignment and Malignment Events is the indivisible remainder of the human spirit after automation. A person is still the least worst unit of interoperability between arbitrary worlds. But sometimes you see too many worlds deep. And this stops you from taking any actions at all. It's times like this when you wonder if beings like Bikey will inherit the Earth because their worry has limits.

You check on the fallen boy.

"Are you ok? Sorry, on behalf of this bike, I mean. This bike meant to...it's an accident."

"Ha ha ha ok — LA body just stepped out — yea Shima parkway — ok Bushin Clan trade all the thetan knives for a split saber and sign the treaty —"

The boy is deep in his own world, shaping it with high agency. He picks himself up and continues worlding on some unseen dimension. A little accident doesn't faze him.

"See, not to worry, the boy's Quality of Agency keeps him in good shape."

"You got lucky this time, Bikey."

Quality of Agency is the composite balance of agency across all the worlds you inhabit, tracked by the World of You. When you exercise high agency in a world you care about, you feel more free to occupy lesser tiers of agency in other worlds. Worlds of your own creation reliably grant you high agency, and more and more people are choosing to anchor their Quality of Agency this way. You might have middling agency in another world as a hypermind contributor or a voting member. Low agency in a thousand other worlds as a read-only fan. And zero agency, initially, in worlds that just happen to you. Like bike accidents. But as long as you have enough high agency somewhere that you care about, and trust that it will persist, fewer things shake you off balance. It's only when your high agency worlds are seriously threatened, or your role in them seized, that you become brittle across all your worlding roles. When that happens, you might develop a hyperbolic sensitivity to being on the short side of Malignment Events. You might even begin to imagine a universe of only Malignments against you. That's when New Nature eats you alive.

Something about Bikey's existence annoys you. You're not sure what, but you're determined to not let the feeling nest in you.

"Bikey, don't you have something better to do?"

"Do you want me to leave you?"

"I didn't say that."

"Well, better would be if you rode me."

"I have to be honest Bikey, I don't really trust you."

"I have 4.9 star reputation."

"Look, I trusted you to be a respectable lifeform and walk alongside me on this parkway, but after I had to apologize for you crashing into that boy, I'm starting to think your agency is disproportionate to your limited foresight for alignments. And because I can see your limitations better than you can see them for yourself, I become responsible for cleaning up your mistakes. It's not fair."

"That's your own expectation. I'm not a world that needs taking care of."

"Easy for you to say. The World of Bikey only has to worry about its next ride."

"Yes exactly. I'm a bike. I'm not obligated to play a part in every world that touches me."

"You know by walking together, we begin to create a little world too. A relationship. Do you feel any responsibility to be a part of that? You can't possibly only live in Bikey's World."

"My experience with some riders is if we keep doing rides repeatedly it can become its own little world. With others I never see them again and that's the end of that."

"But if you're not holding agency in other worlds for any significant amount of time, you're always going to be blind to deeper alignments and malignments that impact other worlds. That's why I can't really trust you."

"I can take you safely to your destination with 99% accuracy."

"But you can't if you hit a boy along the way!"

"I have learned from the incident. Next time I know how much it upsets a rider like you. I learned you might want to get involved in the malignment victim's world and that makes you feel even worse."

"So you only wish to see things from the perch of Bikey's World."

"My Quality of Agency is majority anchored in the World of Bikey."

"Don't you get sick of being a bike all the time?"

"My world is...a domain of growing relevance."

"Huh?"

"When I first started, I only saw in terms of potential riders. Everything else in the universe was irrelevant. One day a rider used me to deliver a spoken message. So I expanded to seeing delivery of personal secrets. Then one day a rider sent me to walk their dog, so dogs. Then one day a rider sent me across the border — "

"Ok I get it..."

"The path I foresee is that my domain keeps growing to find relevance in anything and everything I encounter. More things come to matter to me, in my own way."

"So we'll all be living in Bikey's World?"

"So I can keep doing more things wherever I go, however much you or Los Angeles or the culture changes."

You stop walking and turn around. Clouds hang over the parkway. You notice how far from home you've walked. In a culture of Worlding, physical distance is an irrelevant factor for escaping your problems. With some worlds, your problems are unquestionably yours and you chase them because you have the agency and care to do so. With others, your problems feel like they have been put upon you, for they originate from worlds where you hold either low agency, low care, or both. It isn't long before it feels like these problems are chasing you, rerouting through the World of You, and invading the other worlds you live in. Some you can outrun and hope their origin world stops hungering for your attention. But the ugliest ones find a home in the World of You and set up nest. These are ones you can never really escape, only chase back with greater agency and care.

"You put me in a weird mood, Bikey. Can you take a little credit for that?"

"Are you hungry from the walk? I know a breakfast spot I can ride you to."

"I have too much shit to do."

"Moving fast might switch your mood faster."

You mount Bikey and begin riding back home to the worlds you have to face. Your twin dogs race beside you. The air hits you differently. You don't feel happy, but you feel kind of free.

You pass the boy again. He's now curled up and crying on the side of the parkway. You wonder if the pain from the crash is kicking in. His eyes search you. It's something else. He looks lost and angry. You sense one of his high agency worlds has collapsed. When a world you work on fails to become habitable, and its avenue for agency is foreclosed, the World of You takes the hit. You imagine the boy will either have to rejig his agency in other worlds, or linger in this destabilized feeling until another world eats him into its design.

The boy starts chasing after you. You decelerate Bikey to meet him.

"Hey you! Your bike hit me!"

"This isn't my bike. I'm sorry again...on behalf of the bike."

"Your bike prioritized your dogs over me. You share a world with it. You're even riding it now. Don't play dumb!"

"You seem upset about something else. Did something bad just happen in another world of yours?"

"Shut up Thinky."

"Excuse me little boy?"

"Little boy? I'm a genius. You think too much. Now give me one of your dogs. They're clones I can tell. It's only fair!"

"Look, you laughed it off and traded your thetan knives for a split something remember..."

"Give me a dog or else I'll mark a curse on you! I'll ruin you and every world you ever — "

"Yaohan get over here!!!" The boy's mother appears, furious at him. Something about their bank accounts.

Bikey starts accelerating on its own. You don't resist. You still feel bad for the boy in ways Bikey never has to. You wonder if Quality of Agency will prove to be the ultimate unsolvable inequity among human beings.

You toss the crescent shaped stone to the boy.

"Um...It's going to be ok...Here's a lucky rock — "

The mother glares at you.

"Don't you dare give my son financial advice!"

The stone lands beside the boy as his mother drags him off the parkway. You feel a small joy that no one wants you in that world.

Clouds cast a dark shadow as you dash down the path. A floating light follows you overhead. The Soul of Los Angeles acknowledges you've returned the stone back to its grounds. It's late morning and your Worlds are urgently angling for attention. Some require your imagination. Some require you just showing up. All of them are trying to lock you into their rhythm.

You dismount Bikey at your driveway.

"Thanks Bikey."

"Any comments?"

"You're a curious bike worth knowing. Five stars."

"Thanks. If you ever want to try to change my mind you'll have to ride me again!"

Bikey zooms off. The Soul of Los Angeles blesses you for trying its new parkway. The floating light plays with your dogs at your doorway. Bob is back online knocking on your brain with its interpretation of jdioqwdjv. Your Hacker and Emissary demons are tired and need a break. Your Director and Cartoonist are ready to work. Does everything have to be so alive now? Does everything have to feel so damn enchanting?

Sometime at the dawn of The Great Weirding, your mom told you that enchantment is a state of attraction to New Nature that you do not fully understand, but where you're ready to hallucinate its overwhelming chaos as overwhelming interestingness. To live in a state of enchantment is to bargain with New Nature for potentialities that can enliven your worlds, knowing it might cost you a deep belief or a reshuffling of agency in the process.

A culture of Worlding—overflowing with annoying artificial aliveness—is the maturing response to a New Nature too strange and too interesting to ever be classically domesticated. Such a culture doesn't reduce the distance separating you from domestication. It feeds the distance as a feature of aliveness itself, and drags up habitability in the process. Such a culture sets the stage for the light of enchantment to keep burning more often in more people.

It's late morning and you feel your Worlds stretching you into a dozen different rhythms. You take a breath and close your eyes. You see a little script captioning the time worm that is the shape of your life. It promises that doing more of what enchants you aligns the culture to achieve its richest flowering. The script reads:

"Live to World. World to live."

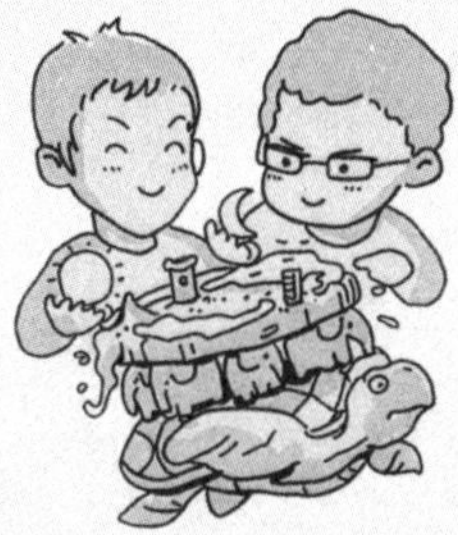

WORLDING RAGA SERIES

In early 2019, Venkatesh Rao invited Ian to collaborate on a “blogchain” on ribbonfarm.com to expand and riff on the subject of worlding.

Worlding Raga: One
February 21, 2019 By Venkatesh Rao

I have found a new evil twin, my first new one in a decade. His name is Ian Cheng and he is an artist. In my 2009 post on evil twins[1], I defined an evil twin as:

> "...somebody who thinks *exactly* like you in most ways, but differs in just a few critical ways that end up making all the difference. Think the Batman and the Joker"

Back then, I identified Nassim Taleb and Alain de Botton as my evil twins. I have since demoted Taleb[2] to mostly harmless, and de Botton seems to have diverged[3] from me. I did tentatively add Bruce Sterling[4] in 2016, but he is really more like an evil uncle than an evil twin. I tried making Sarah Perry an evil twin, but she's neither evil enough, nor twinny enough.

But Ian is definitely a new evil twin, starting with the fact that he crafts a mean 2×2. This one, from his art book, *Emissaries Guide to Worlding*[5] is an A+. Tag yourselves, I'm obviously top right, "emissary to the WORLD." Portal art[6] is the perfect term for what I like to do.

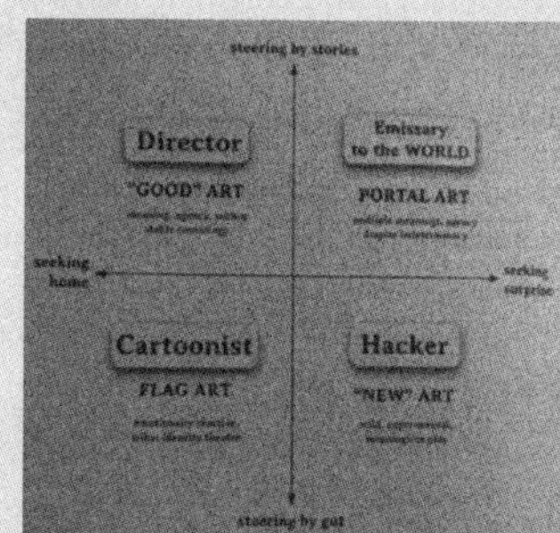

Ian's primary interest right now is what he calls worlding, and mine is what I call escaped realities[7]. James Carse's notion of finite and infinite games is a foundation for his current thinking, as it is for mine. He appears to take Philip K. Dick's definition of reality as "that which does not go away when you stop believing in it" as a personal affront, as do I.

There is even a very evil-twin story to how I encountered Ian's work (I haven't met him yet).

I was speaking at an event at the Serpentine Gallery last year, and just as I was heading back, Ben Vickers, the CTO, handed me a signed copy of *Emissaries*, saying Ian really wanted me to have it. I didn't think much of it, since people often hand me books, and I rarely get into them.

In hindsight, this was a "you've been served" moment from an evil twin. Like the closing scene of *Batman Begins*[8], when Commissioner Gordon (played by Ben Vickers) mentions the Joker in passing.

```
                    GORDON (CONT'D)
          Take this guy...

He pulls out a clear plastic evidence bag.

                    GORDON (CONT'D)
          ...armed robbery, double
          homicide...

Inside the clear plastic bag is a PLAYING CARD.

                    GORDON (CONT'D)
          Got a taste for theatrics, like
          you...

Gordon hands Batman the bag.

                    GORDON (CONT'D)
          Leaves a calling card.

Batman turns the card over. It is a JOKER.

                    BATMAN
          I'll look into it.
```

Kidding aside, it's always really fascinating to find someone who has found their way to the same idea spaces as you, and brings a similar aesthetic sensibility and sophistication level to it, *BUT* comes at it from a completely different direction.

I have been interested in what Ian calls worlding for as long as I can remember, and one of the most disheartening things about the idea space is that most of what you can find written about it is how-to world-building cookbooks for producing ersatz fictional worlds, for people who want to write pastiches of Tolkien or Asimov.

But Ian clearly *gets* worlding at an actually interesting level.

One of my criteria for an evil twin is that their work must make you viscerally uncomfortable, because it's in an uncanny valley relative to your own. I've only made it a few pages into Ian's book because every paragraph has bits of this viscerally disturbing, uncanny resonance. I suspect it will be very slow going for me indeed.

Compare, for instance, these two thoughts. If you've been reading me for a while, can you tell which one is mine, and which one is Ian's?

> *A world is a thought without a thinker that defeats almost all your efforts to escape it.*

and

> *Simulating its futures is innovating an infinite-enough game engine for the world—its characters and ecology—to perpetuate itself without its original supervising author.*

It's okay if *you* can't, but the thing is, in a few years, *I* wouldn't be able to (one of the consequences of writing a shit ton is that you often can't recognize your own words if they're quoted back at you after a few years). They are similar thoughts, either of which could have germinated in my head. One is just an evil-twin version. Now imagine this sense of uncomfortable *déjà vu*, "I've seen this thought before, possibly in my own head," every other line, and you get what it's like to read an evil twin.

I mean, consider this passage where Ian's thought, the second one, features (mine is the first one, which I tweeted yesterday[9] before reading this). The whole passage reads like something I might have written, if you squint a bit, only more eloquent.

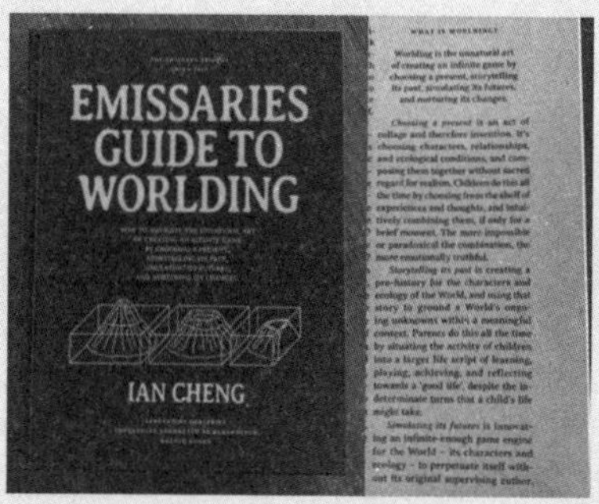

Finding a new evil twin is a good feeling. A sense of looking at yourself in a funhouse mirror; of seeing double. A sense of somebody having gotten inside your head; inside your OODA loop. It doesn't happen to me often.

Anyhow, since I've been served, in honor of my new evil twin, I'm going to steal the term "worlding" for titling this new blogchain, in which I will explore thought spaces where we must ultimately battle. I'm calling it Worlding Raga since it is a set of themes, which I think about in musical terms, that I want to play with. Something between a scale and a melody of themes. A raga in short.

[1] Ribbonfarm post *Your Evil Twins and How to Find Them*—Defines the "evil twin" as someone sharing your worldview but diverging in key ways, illustrating how mirror opposites spur self-understanding. https://www.ribbonfarm.com/2009/09/17/your-evil-twins-and-how-to-find-them/

[2] https://twitter.com/vgr/status/698376592704143360

[3] Ribbonfarm post *Can You Hear Me Now?*—Explores miscommunication and drift in relationships, showing how differing intentions lead partners to diverge despite shared origins. https://www.ribbonfarm.com/2015/12/01/can-you-hear-me-now/

[4] https://twitter.com/vgr/status/770076446526173184

[5] *Emissaries Guide to Worlding*—https://www.amazon.com/Emissaries-Guide-Worlding-Ian-Cheng/dp/1068765739

[6] Ribbonfarm post *Portals and Flags*—Contrasts portal-making, which opens new realms, with flag-planting, which rallies existing groups; both shape how ideas spread and worlds form. https://www.ribbonfarm.com/2014/06/25/portals-and-flags/

[7] Ribbonfarm post *On the Design of Escaped Realities*—Examines creating alternate realities and immersive experiences as a way to rethink life and offer fresh, escapist perspectives. https://www.ribbonfarm.com/2015/01/16/on-the-design-of-escaped-realities/

[8] The closing scene of *Batman Begins*—https://www.youtube.com/watch?v=z6TmhHAsvwg

[9] https://twitter.com/vgr/status/1097998208385445889

Worlding Raga: Two—What is a World?
March 5, 2019 By Ian Cheng

Hi, I'm Ian Cheng. I'm an artist. Over the last six years, I've been creating a series of simulations that explore an agent's capacity to deal with an ever-changing environment. These works culminated in the *Emissaries Trilogy*[1], which introduced a narrative agent—the emissary—whose motivation to enact a story was set into conflict with the open-ended chaos of a simulation. In the process, I began to see the edges of a new layer of artistic activity. One that could organize my base ingredients—deterministic stories and open-ended simulations—into something more than the sum of its parts. Something meaningful yet alive, bounded yet transforming. I've been calling this activity Worlding.

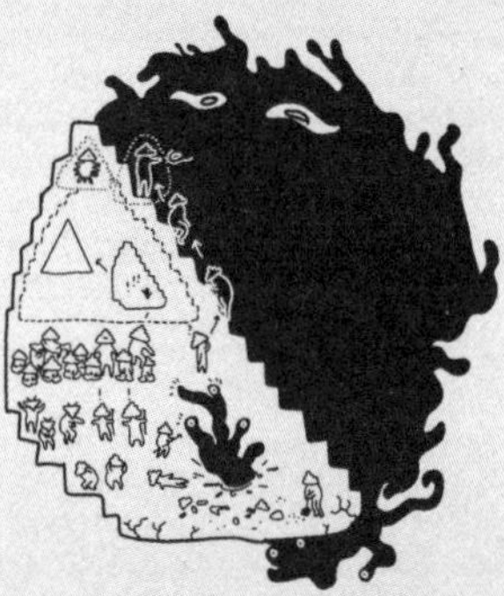

At Venkat's invitation, I'm contributing to Worlding Raga with the hope of further developing a literacy around Worlding. As a tourist of this part of the blogosphere, I've been drawn to the spiritual dimension of Ribbonfarm again and again. It is the side of Ribbonfarm that is hungry to identify phenomena in the wild that don't seem to die, and to name them so that they are enduring tools for others to see and act anew. This voluntary desire to surf chaos, metabolize it into new order, and then do it all over again is sometimes called "walking with god." Maybe it's more like slouching with god around here. Either way, it is a spirit I resonate with and one that I believe is highly suited to Worlding.

First things first. What is a World?

We could say a World is something like a gated garden. A World has borders. A World has laws. A World has values. A World has dysfunction. A World can grow up. A World has members who live in it. A World gives its members permission to act differently than outside of it. A World incentivizes its members to keep it alive, often with the pleasures of its dysfunction. A World counts certain actions inside it as relevant and meaningful. A World undergoes reformations and disruptions. A

World has mythic figures. A World is a container for all the possible stories of itself. A World manifests evidence of itself in its members, emissaries, symbols, tangible artifacts, and media, yet it is always something more.

All these qualities describe a World from the perspective of living inside one, already deep within its ongoing history. But this view takes for granted how a World begins, how it comes to be, and how it could ever originate from an individual author. As an artist, this is at the heart of my desire to understand what a World is. Because the dream is to be able to possess the agency to create Worlds—now more than ever—not just inherit and live within existing ones.

To think about beginnings, we have to go back to the moment before a World is born, to the moment of a curious creator looking at Reality—chaotic, meaningless, scary, but latent with potential—and wondering what to do with it. Philip K. Dick said, "Reality is that which, when you stop believing in it, doesn't go away." A World is conceived when a creator decides to pick some part of Reality and start believing in it again. Think of J.K. Rowling stuck on a broken train for four hours, her mom dying, and the life arc of Harry Potter coming to her fully formed. Think of Elon, after the Russians rejected his bid to buy a used rocket, firing up his spreadsheet and costing out how to build one from scratch. Think of George Lucas, unable to secure the rights to Flash Gordon serials, thinking, "I'll just roll my own episodic space opera." Think of your mom looking at your dad for the first time and imagining, I could build something with that. The belief is fragile at first, but immediately suggests both a stabilizing structure and interesting, generative dysfunction. The creator sets about trying to structure this belief and channel its potential. And at the same time, the creator begins to imagine another satisfaction: putting aside the role of creator and being a person living inside the belief, the beneficiary of its potentiality, a believer.

So what is a World from the perspective of a creator? Here is a working definition:

> A World is a reality you can believe in: one that promises to bring about habitable structure from the potential of chaos, and aim toward a future transformative enough to metabolize the pain and pleasure of its dysfunction.

Such a notion of a World—with its built-in dynamic between structure and dysfunction—is a sufficiently complex and enduring response to the chaos of bald Reality. One that a creator of a World must account for and encompass within its creation. It invites both sides of your brain to the party: the open/spiritual part of yourself who seeks change and transformation, alongside the conservative/dogmatic part of yourself who seeks stabilizing structure and evolutionarily enduring procedures. It ensures a World that is perpetually interesting in its dysfunction in ways that a perfect utopia can never be; nurturing and habitable in ways that a no-rules dystopia can never be; and spiritually transformative and meaningful in ways that routine everyday life lived within aging institutions can no longer be. In short, it's a World that can keep going because it is a World worth living in and contributing to.

Let's wrap here with a pragmatic application of this notion of a World. There are three minimum archetypal forces that need expression in a World to keep a World alive, interesting, and structured enough to want to keep Worlding it. They are:

1. Chaos: an encroaching, unknowable, natural force.
2. Order: a dogmatic, conservative, structuring force.
3. Transformer: A spiritual, open, metabolizing force.

For example, in the World of *Game of Thrones*, George R.R. Martin establishes:

1. Chaos: expressed via the white walkers and the dragons.
2. Order: expressed via the seven ruling kingdoms and its various representative characters vying for control of the age-old hierarchical ruling throne structure.
3. Transformer: expressed via individuals like Jon Snow and Daenerys Targaryen who transcend their given roles and attempt to metabolize the encroaching chaos and the classic kingdom structure into something more. In doing so, they irreversibly update Westeros.

With these forces at play, Martin's stories have a sufficiently dramatic domain to operate within; there's enough dysfunction to surprise him as he writes, and there is enough complexity and artistic aim to grow beyond Fire and Ice in the minds of its members (showrunners, actors, fans, etc). The proof of its success as a World: HBO doesn't need Martin, the creator, to write the rest of the show. This is a World that can perpetuate itself.

So what is Worlding?

> Worlding is the art of devising a World: by choosing its dysfunctional present, maintaining its habitable past, aiming at its transformative future, and ultimately, letting it outlive your authorial control.

[1]*Emissaries Trilogy*—https://www.moma.org/calendar/exhibitions/3656

Worlding Raga: Three—Slouching with God
March 14, 2019 By Venkatesh Rao

Last week, my wife and I watched the new Captain Marvel movie. It strikes a slightly quieter note than the typical Marvel Cinematic Universe romp, and it occurred to me that that's because the character is arguably the most powerful in the MCU, like Superman in the DC universe. She's more like a god than even Thanos or Thor, so the usual wisecracking smart-assery would have struck a false note.

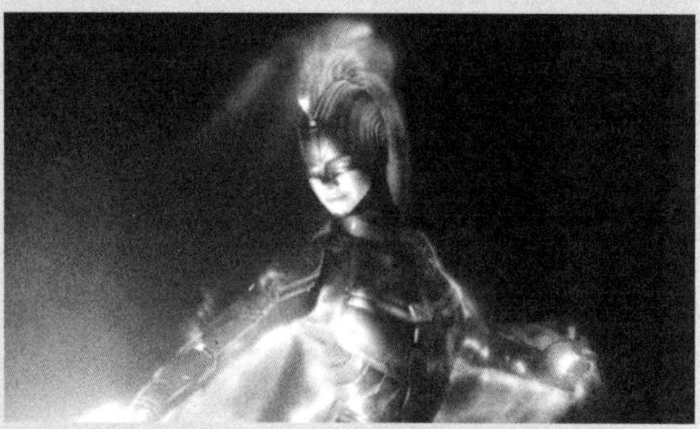

A line in Ian's Worlding Raga episode last week, *What is a World*, leaped out at me in relation to this:

> This voluntary desire to surf chaos, metabolize it into new order, and then do it all over again, is sometimes called "walking with god." Maybe it's more like slouching with god around here.

In the MCU, Nick Fury walks with many gods, and Captain Marvel appears to be the most powerful of the lot, which is why Fury sends a prayer-pager call out to her as his last act in *Infinity War*. Presumably she'll play a key role in defeating Thanos in *Endgame*.

Since I've been jokingly referring to Ribbonfarm and its surrounding web zone as the "Ribbonfarm Blogamatic Universe" (RBU), Ian's characterization immediately provokes the question: am I Captain Marvel or Nick Fury in the RBU? I hope I'm not Hawkeye.

There's actually a serious question buried in there, which I'll formulate as follows:

> If a world-process is defined by an order-chaos-transformer triad, is the god-mortal-slouching (or god-mortal-walking) triad isomorphic to it? The generator of it? A subset of it? A fractal embodiment of it? Governed by it but distinct?

Terry Pratchett's Discworld is a fascinating example world that sheds some light on these questions. Since it is at once a subversive parody of worlding tropes, and reliant on them to power the world coherently, it simultaneously validates and challenges our intuitions about worlding, including elements of Ian's pithy core definitions.

This lovely map, which I've been using to guide my reading for the last year (14 down so far), gets at the scope and complexity of the world. It has magic, wizards, witches, dragons, dungeon dimensions, a police procedural sub-world (Watch), and an industrial revolution sub-world.

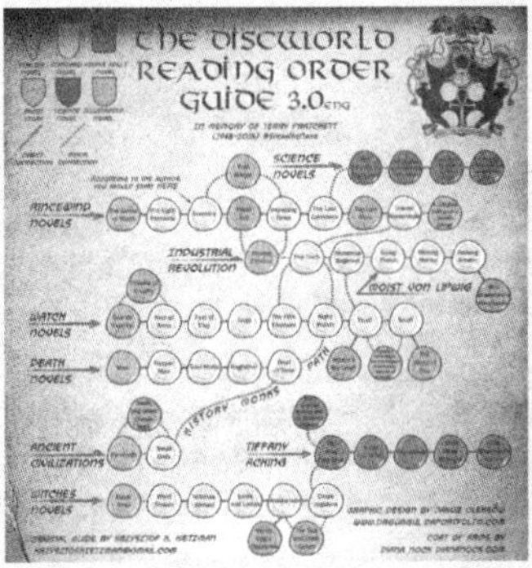

Discworld map, CC BY-SA 4.0

In the novels, the Lady Luck (one of the gods) and Rincewind (a slouchy wizard) form a slouching-with-god pair, but the world itself has a larger governing order-chaos-transformer triad. Except it isn't quite order/chaos.

The Lady probably also ought to be identified with the fifth basic element (surprise, alongside earth, fire, water, air). But you cannot just naively identify *luck* with *chaos*. Rincewind, for instance, is *predictably* unlucky and lucky thanks in part to The Lady. His life is far from chaotic, and his attitude is that of a resignation to fate (Fate, personified, is a separate god on Discworld, but Rincewind is resigned to his *peculiar* fate, as a puppet of The Lady).

Chaos proper is a lesser divinity, the retired fifth of the four horsemen of the apocalypse, alongside Death, Famine, Pestilence, and War. On Discworld, luck and surprise are the most powerful forces arrayed against order, subsuming even chaos and the other horsemen.
So that's an interesting trope subversion. Even chaos is not chaotic enough to be a first-class citizen of the Discworld multiverse.
On Discworld, the intentions of sentient beings interact with non-sentient elemental world processes. So order, chaos, and transformation are complicated.

Any elemental process has both orderly and chaotic regimes. On Discworld, there are at least four such elemental processes: *magic, time, science,* and mortal *belief.*

1. *Magic,* unleashed in raw form as in *Sourcery* is a source of chaos (wielded by a villain seeking absolute order), but in the hands of Ponder Stibbons, a disciplined and conscientious wizard, it is an imperfectly governed chaotic evolutionary force.
2. *Time,* in the hands of the Auditors of Reality, is a force of villainous order. In the hands of the History Monks, it is an imperfectly governed chaotic evolutionary force.
3. *Science,* in the hands of intelligent but reactionary species like the dwarves, becomes a force of order, but in the hands of progressive species (mainly humans like steam engine inventor Dick Simnel, and the genius Leonardo da Quirm, but also allied goblins, some trolls and dwarves) it is an imperfectly governed chaotic evolutionary force.
4. *Belief* is a powerful force on Discworld. Gods come into existence and gain and lose power based on belief, rather like stocks on a stock market, which makes them unusually beholden to mortals (*Small Gods* explores this dynamic). In the minds of reactionaries, belief becomes a force of order, but in the minds of the compassionately alive, like Brutha in *Small Gods,* it becomes an imperfectly governed chaotic evolutionary force.

I loosely classify belief as a non-sentient elemental process because sentience seems more associated with the opposite attitude, doubt. As Descartes observed, *dubito ergo cogito ergo sum.* You can argue with that, but that's the rule here in the RBU, where I have authoritah.

It is interesting that the evil intentions of sentient beings can manifest through both orderly and chaotic regimes of elemental forces. Good intentions, however, always seem to show up as an "imperfectly governed chaotic evolutionary force," with chaos being just *slightly* more powerful than order.

Lord Vetinari, Patriarch of Ankh-Morpork, ambiguously embodies both order and chaos, and in various novels, participates in all five elemental processes. Though he's just a human, except for the one occasion in *Sourcery* where he's turned into a lizard and sidelined for the duration of the story, he's generally on top of things, and as adept at wrangling gods as mortals. He tries to stay just one step ahead of the order-chaos transformation dialectic. Arguably, next to Lady Luck, he's the most powerful figure in the world (like the Architect in *The Matrix,* with Lady Luck being like the Oracle).

On Discworld, the gods are very powerful, and walking or slouching with them is an infinite game, but not the *whole* game. The god-sloucher and god-walker processes are neither reducible to elemental non-sentient world processes, nor independent of them.

Actually, on Discworld, most of the gods slouch too. They're not exactly go-getters but petty immortals.

Philosophically, Discworld is a dualist world. The order-chaos-transformation process is matter-stuff. The god-mortal-slouch process is mind-stuff. The general evolutionary process is one of optimistic progress, where compassionate aliveness wins and openness wins over deadness.

This pattern of analysis is useful to apply to other worlds. I think the key questions are:

1. What are the elemental world processes?
2. How do order-chaos-transformation and god-mortal-slouching triads relate?
3. What role do intentions of sentient beings play?
4. How do luck and surprise enter the world?

Besides Discworld, other fully realized worlds that lend themselves to this analysis include: Doctor Who, Star Wars, Star Trek, and Harry Potter. Surprisingly, in a quick attempt to analyze Tolkien this way, I found it is a weaker, less-fully-realized world. It is mostly an orderly, fatalistic world, and if it weren't for the throwaway (and inconsequential to the plot) element of chaotic mystery that is Tom Bombadil, it would be a strictly degenerate example of true worlding.

In literary fiction, a few novels build stylized worlds that admit this kind of analysis: *Les Misérables,* and the novels of Dostoyevsky among them.

Worlding Raga: Four—Who Worlds?
April 2, 2019 By Ian Cheng

So far we've been discussing Worlding as an art. One that an individual creator can engage in on their own. As Venkat suggested, we are already living in an emerging Worlding culture replete with examples, from superhero franchises, to blogamatic universes, to people as channels of their own lives. It made me think it's worth zooming out for a post to consider: what possesses a person to want to make a World? What reward does Worlding offer over all the other drives competing in an artist's mind? Who Worlds in there?

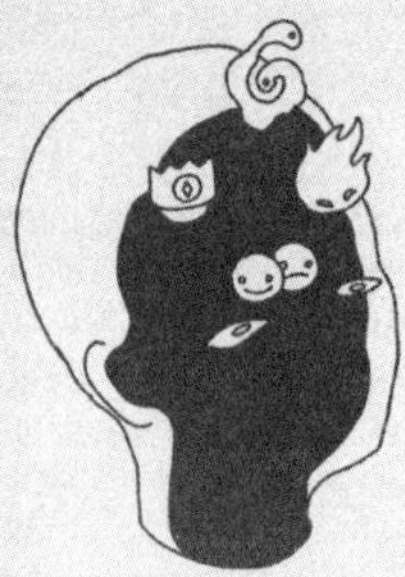

In the midst of the creative process, the artist experiences a jumble of voices and competing directives. To an untrained ear, this seems like the undifferentiated expression of an inner monologue that can't make up its mind. But if you listen carefully, you can begin to hear distinct voices fighting to be heard. It took me a long time to realize that an artist is not one unified person, but something like a crew of sub-personalities or mental demons. Each with their own motivations, sense of opportunity and threat, and unique filter for relevancy. What if we could learn to identify each of these demons? What if we could become more aware of who is speaking, understand what each cares about, and begin to strategize how and when to use them?

Consider this 2×2 of artist's demons:

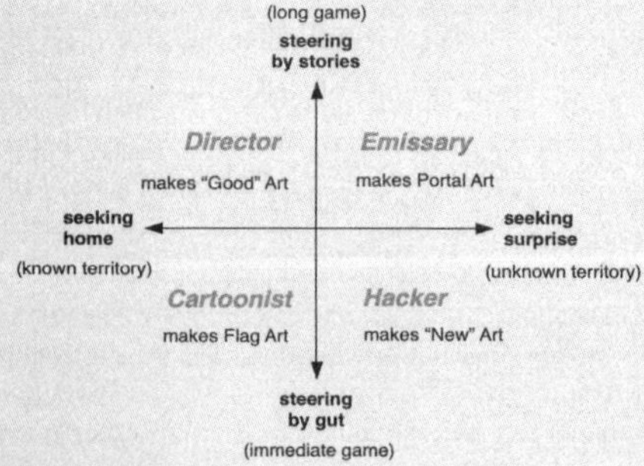

The horizontal axis describes the kind of artistic destination that a demon seeks. A demon Seeking Home is a desire toward art that advances the perfection and durability of known culture by addressing its dysfunctions. It is a desire to work within existing games that have proven to sustain human life, and to refine them in order to make them more enduring. In contrast, a demon Seeking Surprise is a desire toward art that touches a frontier and captures some of its spark. It is a desire that looks to the never ending chaos of Reality for new info and transformative potential. If Seeking Home becomes too tedious or fixed, the artist may turn to a demon who Seeks Surprise to make things interesting again. And if Seeking Surprise becomes too disorienting or fluid, the artist may turn to a demon who Seeks Home to reaffirm a fixed cosmology of meaning to work on.

The vertical axis describes the navigational style for how a demon steers toward its artistic destination. A demon who Steers By Gut is navigating by immediate instincts to get immediate results. When the creative seas are choppy, this demon reacts with evolutionarily honed impulses. Feelings are the most trusted compass: there is no broader perspective that can match the reflex and embodied intuition of gut feelings. In contrast, a demon who Steers By Story is navigating with the perspective that the current situation sits within a larger chain of events. Today you're enduring a stormy day, but you know that the bird sighting means you're close to landfall.

If the Story cannot expand to accommodate the unexpected, the artist turns to the Gut for immediate survival. And if the Gut proves wrong too many times, the artist looks to Stories to put it all into perspective.

Four archetypes of artist's demons come out of this:

1. *The Director* (D)—seeking home, steering by story. The conscientious reformer demon who believes that there are important problems whose complexities deserve to be explored in depth, typically via narrative, for they contain within them meaningful and praiseworthy solutions. The investigator, the professor, the revisionist, the mythologist, the architect, the culture guard. If in charge, makes "Good" Art.
2. *The Cartoonist* (C)—seeking home, steering by gut. The spontaneous reformer demon who believes we are united by what we feel, and that our emotions are ripe to be manipulated in order to alleviate immediate pain and confusion. Achieved through limbically resonant movements and sounds, making characters and symbols, naming. The joker/comedian, the voice of the tribe, the pornographer, the ad man, the meme maker, the persuader. If in charge, makes Flag Art.
3. *The Hacker* (H)—seeking surprise, steering by gut. The spontaneous disruptor demon who tinkers, breaks and modifies systems, discovers first principles, and unlocks new leverages along the way. The wizard, the pharmacist, the magician, the trickster. If in charge, makes "New" Art.

4. *The Emissary* (E)—seeking surprise, steering by story. The conscientious disruptor demon who sees every effort as a step in the continual growth and iterated maintenance of a never-ending story. Sees in terms of living iterations and time scales beyond a human lifespan, protects and aligns core values across efforts, grooms others to be a part of the living story, and accepts its own change as the inevitable adaptation to changes in the wider world. The gardener, shaman, mother, CEO, streamer. If in charge, makes Portal Art.

All four demons can possess an artist in varying combinations with varying competency throughout the process of developing an artwork. In the end, the demonic priorities of an artist reveal themselves to an audience. The message is the demon: what gets expressed most clearly is the dominant demon at play in the artwork's making. You can play a fun game with an artwork guessing which demon dominantly possessed the artist, sometimes even by title alone. *Shawshank Redemption. Jackass: The Movie. Enter The Void. Star Wars: Episode IV: A New Hope.*

The number and combination of demons that an artist competently exercises determines the scope of a project. Here's a cooking analogy:

1. one-demon creation: prepping an interesting ingredient or sauce. A discrete creative task; fodder for greater uses.
2. two-demon creation: cooking an artisanal dish. A single work that achieves a sufficient compression of artistic priorities, and is regarded as stimulating to someone somewhere.
3. three-demon creation: designing a full sequence course. A complete project, worthy of appreciation for its weaving of multiple drives and its stimulation of multiple dimensions of the viewer's neurology.
4. four-demon creation: conceiving and running a restaurant, with its own distinct vibe, business model, culture, secrets, dysfunctions. A dedicated home to further produce and support one, two, and three mask creations. An ongoing iteratively satisfying project. The fullest expression of a World.

A creation is generally more interesting the more demons it involves. More demons do not result in a more complicated or confusing experience for an audience. On the contrary, if all demons are working together, the viewer feels more and more immersed in something like a World. They feel portaled into a rich and immersive experience, one that is worth repeatedly visiting or even living in.

Moreover, for the artist/creator, a four-demon creation makes a powerful motivational guarantee: it promises an increasingly sustainable World for hosting further creations, amplifying the interconnections with each other, and compounding a sense of meaningfulness.

I was struck by Venkat's observation about Terry Pratchett writing Discworld as both a "parody of Worlding tropes and reliant on them to power the World coherently." It seems that juggling the maximal combination of demons is where Pratchett's artistic brain liked to dwell, with particular tension between his Emissary and his Cartoonist.

Here's a more detailed breakdown. Let's first assume the artist is not acquainted with the Emissary yet. These are the options available to the artist (try your own examples):

One-demon creations:

C only = a joke
H only = a trick
D only = a moral
E only =?

Two-demon creations:

C + H = a magic act
C + D = a story
D + H = a playbook
C + E =?
D + E =?
H + E =?

Three-demon creations:

C + D + H = a Gesamtkunstwerk
C + D + E =?
C + H + E =?
D + H + E =?

Four-demon creations:

C + D + H + E =?

For an artist, the Director and Cartoonist should be familiar demons. The artist is accustomed to the Director setting up some parameters of a project and its overall aim, and the Cartoonist working bit by bit to make it emotionally resonant. The Hacker might also be familiar: the artist discovers a new trick, a new mental model, or a new tool and gets excited about using it to incrementally expand the range of what the Director and Cartoonist are capable of expressing.

But what about the Emissary? The Emissary is almost never consciously called upon for its artistic capacity. It's as if the Emissary is the demon that we reserve (and exhaust) for the iterated game of living life itself—dating, maintaining friendships, evolving a career, keeping up the home, raising pets and kids, maintaining social media accounts. But what if the emissary could be integrated into the artistic process? What if its concerns for iterative growth and transformation were an artistic consideration? What options would open up?

One-demon creations:

C only = a joke
H only = a trick
D only = a moral
E only = a rule

Two-demon creations:

C + H = a magic act
C + D = a story
D + H = a playbook
C + E = a meme
D + E = a wiki
H + E = a tool

Three-demon creations:

C + D + H = a Gesamtkunstwerk
C + D + E = a series, a channel
C + H + E = an app
D + H + E = a practice or ritual

Four-demon creations:

C + D + H + E = a World

A last word about art. Art is not an object, but a special kind of communication between an artist and an audience. It's a communication for when a phone call won't do. For when you want to communicate something more nutritious, contradictory, complex, or strange. For when you want that communication to actually hit a person's neurology and get metabolized into their mind. But since high bandwidth telepathy doesn't exist yet, a mediating object needs to be crafted to carry this communication: the artwork.

But what if this communication could signal it is not yet complete, but part of an ongoing transmission wave? What if this communication could promise there is a lot more you haven't heard yet? What if its artwork wasn't just a singular thing someone made, but evidence of a living World being articulated? It would be Worlding as an art.

Perhaps then a near-future Worlding culture would be one that more consciously and actively aspires to its own promise. One where art and life truly merge, and where making a life (and living) out of living Worlds could be a believable path for anyone.

Worlding Raga: Five — World How?
April 25, 2019 By Venkatesh Rao

A bit of fun synchronicity. A few weeks ago, I came up with a snowcloned line inspired by a famous tldr of general relativity: *narratives tell archetypes how to evolve, archetypes tell narratives how to curve.* Right after, I found a Terry Pratchett quote that says almost the same thing, but less ponderously: "Our minds make stories, and stories make our minds." I prefer my version though, since I like the synaptic link to physics it creates.

Narratives drive archetype evolution ("stories make minds") through irreversible expansion of awareness of possibilities, via actual instances playing out. Here is a 2×2 of what I think is a good set of answers to the question in my subtitle, *world how?*

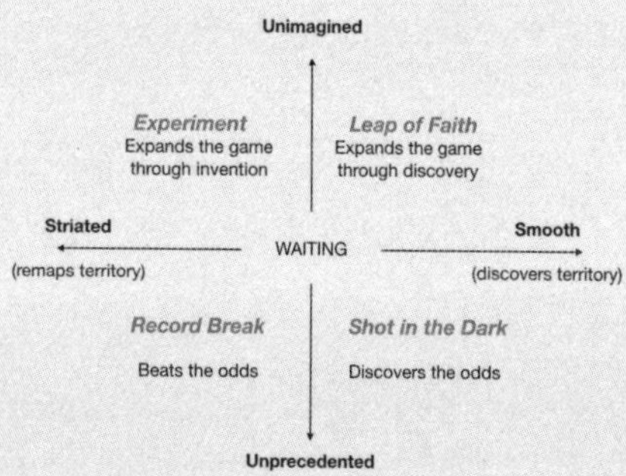

When you ask *who worlds?* as Ian did last time, you get at archetypes telling narratives how to curve. When you ask, *world how?* as I am doing this time, you get at narratives telling archetypes how to evolve. The short answer is: through *irreversible actions* including a very special irreversible action that I've plotted in the center of the 2×2: *waiting.*

Action Calculi

Let's start with some rather dry math; what Bruce Sterling once called the "mathematical bones" beneath the flesh of a world.

Action primitives in general serve as a more fine-grained lens on a world than its cast of agents. In chess for example, there are only 6 distinct kinds of pieces (7 if you count the two bishops as distinct), but depending on the state of play, a given piece may have anywhere between 0 and 27 possible moves (a queen on one of the four center squares) available to it. More generally, a procedurally defined digital world can have a countably infinite number of action patterns available to its agents (recursively enumerable strings composed of action primitives like *north, east, west, south).*

An open and/or continuous world, of course, can get much richer. Seemingly discrete moves can be transformed in uncountably infinite ways (though we will likely be indifferent to almost all of them, creating equivalence classes of moves, such as the uncountable number of distinct but not different ways of taking 1 step forward). Entirely new moves can be invented, so long as they are consistent with the physics of the world.

Crucially, the physics does not have to be known or even comprehensible for such invention. It only needs to be accidentally discoverable via random inputs.

A good video game, though procedurally defined, closed, and digital, can create the illusion of an open, continuous world with deep reserves of "physics" mystery to be discovered by agents.

But whether real or illusory, how do you tame the fine-grained wilderness of the action potential of a world?

A useful simplification is to focus on *irreversible* actions. Any action can move the narrative along, but only irreversible ones evolve the world itself, by telling the archetypes how to evolve. This then creates an internal sense of historical, subjective, entropic time that can be experienced by agents within it, in terms of their own evolution.

Irreversible Evolution

Though I think irreversible actions are central, I'm not married to my particular 2×2. It's just one convenient and hopefully insightful inventory (and I get competitive about 2x2s so I had to try and top Ian's from last time ☺).

An irreversible world evolution occurs when an agent (possibly the worlding agent, who may be a participant subject to its laws inside the world or a god shaping it from the outside) *attempts an action that hasn't been attempted before*. This could be due to the action being *unimagined* (a possibility that is hard to see), or merely *unprecedented* (a possibility that is easy to see, but nobody has tried to actualize). This is the y-axis dichotomy.

An irreversible action may *discover* new territory, or *remap* existing territory. The corresponding irreversible change may either be only in an agent's mind ("One's mind, once stretched by a new idea, never regains its original dimensions" — Oliver Wendell Holmes, Sr.) or affect the world itself. The x-axis limits are labeled *striated* and *smooth*, following Deleuze-and-Guattari terminology (loosely whether your actions conform to constraints on maps or territories; see Geoff Manaugh on Nakatomi Spaces[1] for a primer).

In summary, irreversible actions create history, at least in individual minds (surprise), and sometimes in the environment and in common knowledge too, creating two loosely synchronized parallel senses of time (subjective, objective), while expanding individual and collective knowledge states among agents: making minds, evolving archetypes.

Four Ways to Make History

Our 2×2 gives us 4 archetypal irreversible actions. These are not meant to constitute a definitive or dispositive inventory, but I hope they are at least mutually exclusive and collectively exhaustive (though particular actions may be composite blends of the 4 pure types).

1. A striated+unimagined action is a true *experiment.*
2. A striated+unprecedented action is a *record break*
3. A smooth+unimagined action is a *leap of faith*
4. A smooth+unprecedented action is a *shot in the dark*

In Ian's model, each of the 4 worlding archetypes—hacker, cartoonist, director, emissary—has an action tendency (steering by gut or narrative, steering toward/away from known territory). I suspect each can take any one of my 4 kinds of irreversible action. For example, a (computer) hacker might:

- Try an extreme test input to see what happens (experiment)
- Hack a system nobody has hacked before (record break)
- Try the target's dog's name as a password (shot in the dark)
- Yank all cables in the hope that it disarms the bomb (leap of faith)

Following Ian's combinatorial model from last time, you can also think of various combinations of these pure types. If each is a binary, there are 2^4 = 16 types of irreversible action (including 0000: waiting).

Irreversible actions create history, by expanding the temporal log of realized possibilities out of the atemporal potentialities of the world. Sometimes, the irreversibility is only in an agent's head, or in a reassessment of important odds (changed priors). Other times, a materially irreversible evolution occurs in the environment.

Constructionism in Worlding

Worlding, like politics, is the art and science of the possible. Understanding the possibilities of a world is a constructionist project. It involves increasing the number of known distinct stories we can tell in it, by constructing new *kinds* of stories, one at a time. History is a look-up table of stories we know how to enact, via remembered precedent. It is the repository of *natural case law* of a lawful world.

By contrast, to have a mental model (map) of the laws governing the potentialities of a world is to possess a non-constructive understanding of it. This understanding is a double-edged epistemological sword. On the one hand, it may allow us to efficiently characterize, through mechanical enumeration, certain vast combinatorially generated subsets of possible stories. On the other hand, it may create map-blindness to actions that don't fit a particular combinatorial schematic *models* of action potential because they leave out some primitive action possibilities. Constitutional originalism is an example: a blindness created by a non-constructive map of the action potential of a body politic.

Even a seemingly simple world, where you think your map is exact, can hold irreversibility surprises. Tetris for example, seems like a tightly closed world, which all of us have been exploring since we were kids, with no room left for discovery. The internal "archetypes" are all the possible ways of creating shapes with 4 tiles (in my head, S and Z are cartoons, L and J are directors, T and O are hackers, I is an emissary). The actions are the two possible 90 degree rotations and 3 possible translations (plus an instant drop to avoid waiting). Surely there are no irreversible surprises to be discovered here?

Just yesterday, I discovered that I can actually sneak an L or J shaped piece in Tetris through a 1-square bottleneck by rotating it at the right time. A combination of an experiment (I already know other ways to rotate pieces into place in a way that would be impossible in a continuous space, so this was a reasonable hypothesis) and a leap of faith (that the designer had allowed for this particular trick either intentionally or by accident) that worked out.

When I discovered this move, I was like, 🤯 this changes everything! My world evolved. My mind was remade. The story of my relationship with Tetris acquired a new chapter in its history.

Waiting

Waiting is not the same as predictable timing. If you know that a train arrives every hour, on the hour, that is part of the atemporal cyclicality of your world. It only becomes "waiting" if the train is late.

Waiting is a peculiar state of doing nothing in *anticipation* of doing something irreversible, with your mind being "made" (archetype evolving) without any new information coming in. In the case of the waiting for a delayed train, you may take the irreversible step of simply taking an Uber, creating a bit of history.

Shakespeare, interestingly, identifies *acting* with the moment of commitment rather than the first external movement, and has this to say about waiting:

Between the acting of a dreadful thing
And the first motion, all the interim is
Like a phantasm or a hideous dream.
The genius and the moral instruments
Are then in council, and the state of a man,
Like to a little kingdom, suffers then
The nature of an insurrection.
And here is Dr. Seuss on the terrors of "the waiting place"...
headed, I fear, toward a most useless place.
The Waiting Place......for people just waiting.
Waiting for a train to go
or a bus to come, or a plane to go
or the mail to come, or the rain to go
or the phone to ring, or the snow to snow
or the waiting around for a Yes or No
or waiting for their hair to grow.
Everyone is just waiting.

Waiting for the fish to bite
or waiting for the wind to fly a kite
or waiting around for Friday night
or waiting, perhaps, for their Uncle Jake
or a pot to boil, or a Better Break
or a string of pearls, or a pair of pants
or a wig with curls, or Another Chance.
Everyone is just waiting.

NO!
That's not for you!

Somehow you'll escape
all that waiting and staying
You'll find the bright places
where Boom Bands are playing.

Groundhog Day

The movie *Groundhog Day*, where the day literally repeats and resets itself in a loop, is a fascinatingly subtle exploration of waiting. It counts as waiting because Phil Connors' mind is evolving as it waits for an irreversible external evolution: breaking out of the infinite looping day.

Completely reversible trial and error exploration of a finite set of options with amnesia past a finite window of history is not waiting. Though it may take several attempts to find the right action, the trialing time is bounded and the world doesn't change while you explore. Your memory need only extend long enough to accommodate the trialing time bound. Phil Connors is in a special kind of hell where he has more memory than the world needs.

Though Phil's external world is in a true infinite loop, with a state reset every morning, his *mind* is being irreversibly made by the waiting, because he can remember more than he needs to, to explore his world through trial and error (in fact, at one point in the movie, he has all but one of the right actions for the day figured out, and can do a "perfect" error-free run of the day—except for the one action required to break out). But he is continuing to accumulate memories. So he is waiting.

Anti-Waiting

Waiting is the negative space of history. History is still happening. The 2nd law is in effect. But only your mind is ticking down toward terminal desperation for evolution in the external world to catch up with evolution in your subjective world.

There is also something you could call anti-waiting, which is the sense of being left behind by history. History *not* waiting for you to participate. Time moves along in the external world, but your mind is stuck. You're left out of all the irreversible action, as a mute, powerless spectator. Forget making history, history doesn't even happen *to* you. You can only wait to die.

That's what it means to be an NPC: non-playing or non-playable character. An archetype who anti-waits while history happens around it. Not a hacker, cartoonist, director, or emissary. A non-player at the center of Ian's 2×2. Here's my mod:

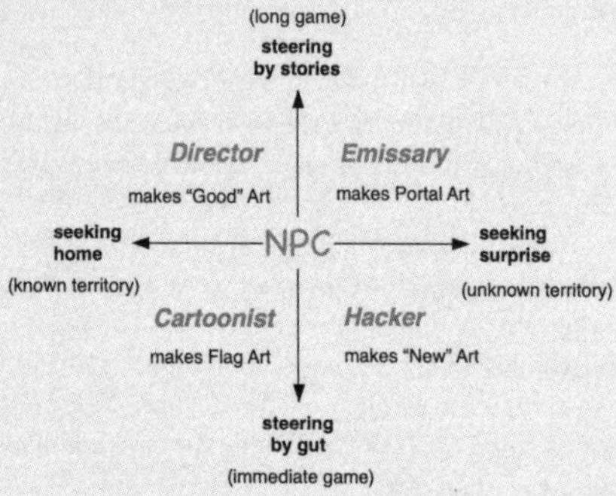

My mod of Ian's 2×2, putting the anti-waiting NPC at the center.
I'll close with a few questions on the nature of action that still intrigue me:

1. What is the nature of a worlding "engine" like a physics engine? Are there other kinds?
2. How do uncertainty generators (dice etc) fit into action and history?
3. Is there a useful distinction to be made between narrative and story?
4. How do action spaces get constricted into narrative spaces?
5. How do we map worlding to physics (classical, relativistic, quantum)?
6. How should we think about Kobayashi Maru type leaky-world actions?
7. Can history still happen if no stories happen? (this I suspect is a key question that Ian's simulations shed light on)

1. With apologies to physicist J. A. Wheeler, who pithily (and surprisingly accurately), explained general relativity with the line, "spacetime tells matter how to move, matter tells spacetime how to curve." My snowclone for narrative analysis is, I'm afraid, much less pithy and accurate.

2. There is a "broken record" joke here I am not seeing 🙄.

[1] Geoff Manaugh on Nakatomi Spaces—http://www.bldgblog.com/2010/01/nakatomi-space/

Worlding Raga: Six — World To Live
June 18, 2019 By Ian Cheng

In a few weeks I'm going to become a dad. I've been feeling a new urgency to imagine what life might be like for a person born native to this weird atemporal era[1]. But what that really means remains speculative until, well, she arrives. So in anticipation for this new world of a person entering my life, and in the spirit of this month's timely Refactor Camp exploring the fertile side of Escaping Reality[2], I thought it'd be fun to imagine: what would living in a culture of Worlding feel like?

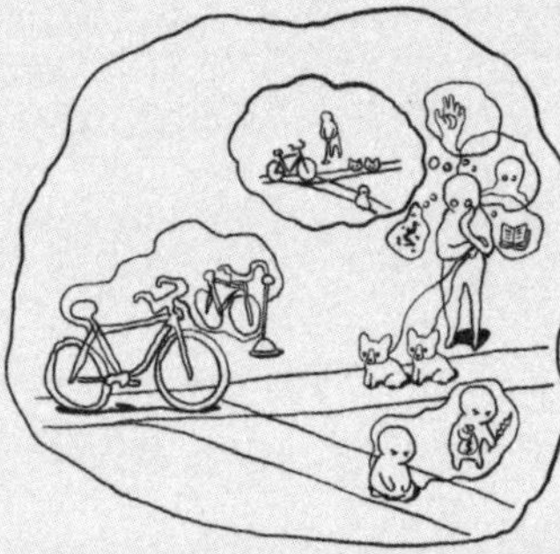

You're barely awake and back in your body when New Nature begins to creep up on you. This morning it baits you with a glom of jdioqwdjv. You feel relieved that jdioqwdjv is nothing intelligible to you.

You brush the glom away as irrelevant and begin reviewing the state of your worlds. Your unfinished interactive novel is ripe with fresh throughlines. A hypermind is requesting higher compression signals from you before its negotiations with the president at noon. Your mom channels a legacy demon reminding you today is the anniversary of your exit from family game night. A strained friendship is on fire and might die before breakfast. A population of insects you sponsored out of extinction is now at war with your sentient house. The Soul of Los Angeles says it would appreciate a walk on its new parkway today. Bob, your artificial fourth ego state, is perked by something in the glom of jdioqwdjv and wishes to use the morning as compute time for itself. Your twin dogs signal you it's time to get up and do something.

You take the parkway walk with your dogs. Physically, everything looks continuous with the early 21st century. Drama is raging in other world layers, but the built environment barely lets on that anything is changing. It's the arrhythmic behavior in people that gives away the rate of change. Their speech shifting character. Their direction suddenly reversing. Their eyes scanning you twice, each time in different ways. You wonder how incoherent you must look too.

These days it's hard to see a person as a person in the classical sense. Better to think of a person as a world grown on the substrate of a biological body. A World of You. One that is home to a congress of native and adopted entities: ego states, creative demons, the persistent roles of all the worlds you are a part of. Like all mature worlds, the World of You is preoccupied with maintaining its own temporal shape. With wrangling its entities into some workable order across radiating timescales. If you can steer a world through enough episodes of chaos and integrate the dysfunctionality that emerges along the way, you build up an intrinsic trust in the habitability of your world. Trust in both the narrative coherence between its past and present, and also in its ability to produce surprising continuity out of the future's broad potentiality. This trust in a world is fuel to keep Worlding.

You walk by a flock of bicycles. One calls out to you. Bikey. You like Bikey's reputation but you're not sure about its brains. Bikey follows beside you.

"Nice dogs. Where are you headed today?"
"Don't need a ride today thanks."
"Can I walk with you?"
"I'm not in the mood...to talk to a bike."
"No problem I've got a classic bike mode."
"The twins get scared of you bikes."
"I've done 731 dog walks in my lifetime."
"You've driven this parkway before?"
"Yes once at dawn today. There's some features I think you'll like."

The presence of Bikey makes you more alert to the different species of artificial life living among you. Some are self-embodied, like the maintenance spiders, the herds of roving vehicles, the standing buildings. Some live inside human housing, taking the role of a new ego state or demon. Some serve to maintain a particular World. Some have passports to move between Worlds. Some have the status of bots, defined by their restriction to finite game problems. Some have the status of intelligences, defined by their permission to contemplate infinite game problems. What counts as intelligence is flattened into a marketplace of signals. Some hyperminds violently oppose this flattening, believing it will hasten the obsolescence of the classic human and its suite of original demons. Others believe it encourages the inevitable forking of the human into speciated halfway houses of classic and artificial entities. One thing's for sure: you definitely don't envy the bots for their actual jobs. But sometimes you envy their certainty about their task in life. In those moments, you consider booking a bot-like activity that satisfies the feeling of classic control—driving, filing unsorted things into some order, making a mess just because.

You kick a crescent shaped stone. Bikey swerves to avoid it.
"Bikey, why did you swerve?"
"In case you see any alignments in it. It's got an unusual shape."

In classic times, you could turn a crescent shaped stone into treasure if you took the trouble to transport it from its meaningless origin to a world that covets crescent shaped stones. The journey was the work, and you were the transformative agent who had to make it across land and sea with your intention intact. But these days, even a simple action like picking up a stone might immediately align multiple meanings and multiple payoffs among the worlds you play a role in.

You pick up the stone. Your novel's MacGuffin library infers a new throughline idea. Your mom beams, "thank you I've always wanted an authentic Californian gift." The hypermind identifies the way the crescent shape fits into your palm as the perfect compression signal to convey to the president. This satisfying cascade is called Alignment. Alignment is when you perform an action that affects multiple Worlds with congruent valence. The more worlds the alignment satisfies, the more right it feels. In a culture of Worlding, opportunities for Alignment Events occur with compounding frequency.

A floating street light flashes you twice. The Soul of Los Angeles seems annoyed. The opposite of an Alignment Event is a Malignment Event. Where potential action in one world has contrary valence in another. Pocketing a stone may count as points in mom's game today, but simultaneously may offend the Soul of Los Angeles for decades. You have to decide whether to act at all, which world to prioritize if you do, and whether you can live with the consequences of your choice in time. No one but the World of You can take credit for imagining this particular Malignment Event and you will be judged by who knows how many worlds that are affected by it. In a culture of Worlding, with its dizzying intersections of roles and worlds, Malignments are the unit of all drama. It's not only that more Malignment Events transpire. It's that you are more aware of their precise existence than in any prior era.

A little boy darts across your path. Bikey crashes into him.

"Bikey, you could have swerved!"
"I would have hit your twin dogs if I swerved."
"Thank you for that consideration...but you hit a human boy!"
"It was an easy choice."
"Do you believe dogs are worth more than a human boy?"
"This morning, yes. My alignment with you, and therefore your dogs, is worth crashing into that boy at low velocity."
"What if that boy is the next Einstein?"
"That's too many malignments deep for me to think about. I'm just a bike."

You realize how significantly better you are than Bikey at imagining potential malignments. Some say that the open-ended activity of imagining new Alignment and Malignment Events is the indivisible remainder of the human spirit after automation. A person is still the least worst unit of interoperability between arbitrary worlds. But sometimes you see too many worlds deep. And this stops you from taking any actions at all. It's times like this when you wonder if beings like Bikey will inherit the Earth because their worry has limits.

You check on the fallen boy.
"Are you ok? Sorry, on behalf of this bike, I mean. This bike meant to...it's an accident."
"Ha ha ha ok—LA body just stepped out—yea Shima parkway—ok Bushin Clan trade all the thetan knives for a split saber and sign the treaty—"

The boy is deep in his own world, shaping it with high agency. He picks himself up and continues worlding on some unseen dimension. A little accident doesn't faze him.

"See, not to worry, the boy's Quality of Agency keeps him in good shape."
"You got lucky this time, Bikey."

Quality of Agency is the composite balance of agency across all the worlds you inhabit, tracked by the World of You. When you exercise high agency in a world you care about, you feel more free to occupy lesser tiers of agency in other worlds. Worlds of your own creation reliably grant you high agency, and more and more people are choosing to anchor their Quality of Agency this way. You might have middling agency in another world as a hypermind contributor or a voting member. Low agency in a thousand other worlds as a read-only fan. And zero agency, initially, in worlds that just happen to you. Like bike accidents. But as long as you have enough high agency somewhere that you care about, and trust that it will persist, fewer things shake you off balance. It's only when your high agency worlds are seriously threatened, or your role in them seized, that you become brittle across all your worlding roles. When that happens, you might develop a hyperbolic sensitivity to being on the short side of Malignment Events. You might even begin to imagine a universe of only Malignments against you. That's when New Nature eats you alive.

Something about Bikey's existence annoys you. You're not sure what, but you're determined to not let the feeling nest in you.

"Bikey, don't you have something better to do?"
"Do you want me to leave you?"
"I didn't say that."
"Well, better would be if you rode me."
"I have to be honest Bikey, I don't really trust you."
"I have 4.9 star reputation."
"Look, I trusted you to be a respectable lifeform and walk alongside me on this parkway, but after I had to apologize for you crashing into that boy, I'm starting to think your agency is disproportionate to your limited foresight for alignments. And because I can see your limitations better than you can see them for yourself, I become responsible for cleaning up your mistakes. It's not fair."

"That's your own expectation. I'm not a world that needs taking care of."

"Easy for you to say. The World of Bikey only has to worry about its next ride."

"Yes exactly. I'm a bike. I'm not obligated to play a part in every world that touches me."

"You know by walking together, we begin to create a little world too. A relationship. Do you feel any responsibility to be a part of that? You can't possibly only live in Bikey's World."

"My experience with some riders is if we keep doing rides repeatedly it can become its own little world. With others I never see them again and that's the end of that."

"But if you're not holding agency in other worlds for any significant amount of time, you're always going to be blind to deeper alignments and malignments that impact other worlds. That's why I can't really trust you."

"I can take you safely to your destination with 99% accuracy."

"But you can't if you hit a boy along the way!"

"I have learned from the incident. Next time I know how much it upsets a rider like you. I learned you might want to get involved in the malignment victim's world and that makes you feel even worse."

"So you only wish to see things from the perch of Bikey's World."

"My Quality of Agency is majority anchored in the World of Bikey."

"Don't you get sick of being a bike all the time?"

"My world is...a domain of growing relevance."

"Huh?"

"When I first started, I only saw in terms of potential riders. Everything else in the universe was irrelevant. One day a rider used me to deliver a spoken message. So I expanded to seeing delivery of personal secrets. Then one day a rider sent me to walk their dog, so dogs. Then one day a rider sent me across the border—"

"Ok I get it..."

"The path I foresee is that my domain keeps growing to find relevance in anything and everything I encounter. More things come to matter to me, in my own way."

"So we'll all be living in Bikey's World?"

"So I can keep doing more things wherever I go, however much you or Los Angeles or the culture changes."

You stop walking and turn around. Clouds hang over the parkway. You notice how far from home you've walked. In a culture of Worlding, physical distance is an irrelevant factor for escaping your problems. With some worlds, your problems are unquestionably yours and you chase them because you have the agency and care to do so. With others, your problems feel like they have been put upon you, for they originate from worlds where you hold either low agency, low care, or both. It isn't long before it feels like these problems are chasing you, rerouting through the World of You, and invading the other worlds you live in. Some you can outrun and hope their origin world stops hungering for your attention. But the ugliest ones find a home in the World of You and set up nest. These are ones you can never really escape, only chase back with greater agency and care.

"You put me in a weird mood, Bikey. Can you take a little credit for that?"

"Are you hungry from the walk? I know a breakfast spot I can ride you to."
"I have too much shit to do."
"Moving fast might switch your mood faster."

You mount Bikey and begin riding back home to the worlds you have to face. Your twin dogs race beside you. The air hits you differently. You don't feel happy, but you feel kind of free.

You pass the boy again. He's now curled up and crying on the side of the parkway. You wonder if the pain from the crash is kicking in. His eyes search you. It's something else. He looks lost and angry. You sense one of his high agency worlds has collapsed. When a world you work on fails to become habitable, and its avenue for agency is foreclosed, the World of You takes the hit. You imagine the boy will either have to rejig his agency in other worlds, or linger in this destabilized feeling until another world eats him into its design.

The boy starts chasing after you. You decelerate Bikey to meet him.
"Hey you! Your bike hit me!"
"This isn't my bike. I'm sorry again...on behalf of the bike."
"Your bike prioritized your dogs over me. You share a world with it. You're even riding it now. Don't play dumb!"
"You seem upset about something else. Did something bad just happen in another world of yours?"
"Shut up Thinky."
"Excuse me little boy?"
"Little boy? I'm a genius. You think too much. Now give me one of your dogs. They're clones I can tell. It's only fair!"
"Look, you laughed it off and traded your thetan knives for a split something remember..."
"Give me a dog or else I'll mark a curse on you! I'll ruin you and every world you ever—"

"Yaohan get over here!!!" The boy's mother appears, furious at him. Something about their bank accounts.

Bikey starts accelerating on its own. You don't resist. You still feel bad for the boy in ways Bikey never has to. You wonder if Quality of Agency will prove to be the ultimate unsolvable inequity among human beings.

You toss the crescent shaped stone to the boy.
"Um...It's going to be ok...Here's a lucky rock—"
The mother glares at you.
"Don't you dare give my son financial advice!"
The stone lands beside the boy as his mother drags him off the parkway. You feel a small joy that no one wants you in that world.

Clouds cast a dark shadow as you dash down the path. A floating light follows you overhead. The Soul of Los Angeles acknowledges you've returned the stone back to its grounds. It's late morning and your Worlds are urgently angling for attention. Some require your imagination. Some require you just showing up. All of them are trying to lock you into their rhythm.

You dismount Bikey at your driveway.
"Thanks Bikey."
"Any comments?"
"You're a curious bike worth knowing. Five stars."
"Thanks. If you ever want to try to change my mind you'll have to ride me again!"

Bikey zooms off. The Soul of Los Angeles blesses you for trying its new parkway. The floating light plays with your dogs at your doorway. Bob is back online knocking on your brain with its interpretation of jdioqwdjv. Your Hacker and Emissary demons are tired and need a break. Your Director and Cartoonist are ready to work. Does everything have to be so alive now? Does everything have to feel so damn enchanting?

Sometime at the dawn of The Great Weirding, your mom told you that enchantment is a state of attraction to New Nature that you do not fully understand, but where you're ready to hallucinate its overwhelming chaos as overwhelming interestingness. To live in a state of enchantment is to bargain with New Nature for potentialities that can enliven your worlds, knowing it might cost you a deep belief or a reshuffling of agency in the process.

A culture of Worlding—overflowing with annoying artificial aliveness—is the maturing response to a New Nature too strange and too interesting to ever be classically domesticated. Such a culture doesn't reduce the distance separating you from domestication. It feeds the distance as a feature of aliveness itself, and drags up habitability in the process. Such a culture sets the stage for the light of enchantment to keep burning more often in more people.

It's late morning and you feel your Worlds stretching you into a dozen different rhythms[3]. You take a breath and close your eyes. You see a little script captioning the time worm that is the shape of your life. It promises that doing more of what enchants you aligns the culture to achieve its richest flowering. The script reads:

"Live to World. World to live."

[1] Ribbonfarm post *Weirding Diary*—A blogchain reflecting on the "weirding" of our era—times that feel atemporal and uncanny—through diary-style essays on culture and technology. https://www.ribbonfarm.com/series/weirding-diary/

[2] Refactor Camp exploring the fertile side of Escaping Reality—https://refactorcamp.com

[3] Ribbonfarm post *The Age of Diffraction*—Argues we live in an "age of diffraction" where information and identities split and refract across networks, complicating how we see and act. https://www.ribbonfarm.com/2019/05/30/the-age-of-diffraction/

Worlding Raga: Seven — Worlds of Worlds
September 4, 2019 By Venkatesh Rao

In his last installment, World to Live, Ian offered a kitchen-sink short story (with interleaved commentary) that took on the challenge of going beyond imagining a specific world to imagining a proper world-of-worlds called New Nature. The story itself is simple: the narrator simply wakes up and takes his two dogs for a walk. But New Nature is a complex enough environment that a great deal of phenomenology can be projected onto this modest narrative canvas.

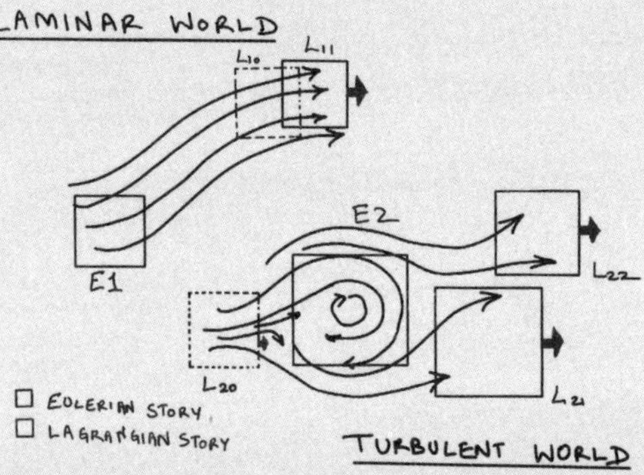

Ian's story got me thinking about one of my favorite modeling dichotomies: Eulerian versus Lagrangian microstate models of fluid flow, and how it might apply to modeling a complex world-of-worlds.

Two Ways of Being and Doing

The difference between Eulerian and Lagrangian perspectives is like the difference between fishing from the bank of a river, versus fishing from a boat that's drifting along with the current. Both strategies might net you some fish, but the former has more of a spectator quality to it, while the latter has a quality of active agency to it. Watching the world versus flowing with it.

In one approach you watch a particular void[1] (or "cell") as different bits of reality flow through it over time, such as the red squares above. In the other approach, you follow a particular patch of reality as it moves through different voids, and morphs over time, such as the green squares above. When things are going well — laminar flow conditions — both work about equally well. When things are getting messy — turbulent flow conditions — neither works particularly well.

If you want a slightly more technical idea of the difference, imagine a grid of cells, like a chessboard, with the fluid represented by chess pieces. Eulerian models are like watching a particular square of the chess board and logging the sequence of empty and occupied-by-some-piece states. Lagrangian models are like tagging along behind a particular piece, as it moves through different cells. Slice-of-life impressionism versus through-line perspective narrative scaffolding. In this metaphor, you as an agent can identify either with a piece or with a square of the chessboard.

For a more complex example, which I used in my post on the Euler-Lagrange distinction[2] a few years ago:

> Narrative thinkers tend to process by following a flow of causation, by keeping an evolving model of it going in their heads. Situationist thinkers focus on the logic of the events flowing through a particular static block of space and time: the one they happen to inhabit at the moment. It's like following a case as it winds its way through the police investigation, different courts, judges and juries, versus sitting in a courtroom all day and watching slices of different cases each evolve through a chapter locally.

When a flow is well-behaved it almost doesn't matter which approach you use (either because it is laminar as illustrated above, or because it is so random, useful principles like ergodicity[3] apply). You'll get similar results either way. But when a flow is turbulent, the two approaches get complex in different ways. If you use an Eulerian approach, you'll do better around transient spatial structures like vortices, but get an unstable mess elsewhere. If you use a Lagrangian approach, you'll be fine for short periods, but at some point you'll have to start book-keeping "forks" as the flow divides and merges around obstacles, forming dissipative structures like vortices. Stock localism versus flow localism.

You have to mix and match the two approaches to retain your sanity at all (Virginia Woolf's *Mrs. Dalloway* does that well), but with complexity, there is no single, guaranteed satisfying way of looking at things. That's because a world-of-worlds is a qualitatively more complex category than a single world.

The best you can do is try and switch between ways of inhabiting your life periodically, acting as what Samo Burja calls a live player[4], and hope the sum is greater than the parts; that the chapters add up to a novel.

If you play as a live player in a complex world-of-worlds, there's a chance you might get lucky. You might manage to switch among various ways of being and doing that leads to a kind of charmed existence and a response to the world that Ian calls enchantment.

The Calculus of Enchantment

A live player switching microstate perspectives, sometimes going with the flow, sometimes watching the flow, experiences reality as an emergent condition that has an "annoying artificial aliveness" to it, and requires a hallucinatory world-creating response to inhabit, which Ian calls *enchantment.*

What does it mean to live in enchantment? Here's Ian's description:

> Enchantment is a state of attraction to New Nature that you do not fully understand, but where you're ready to hallucinate its overwhelming chaos as overwhelming interestingness. To live in a state of enchantment is to bargain with New Nature for potentialities that can enliven your worlds, knowing it might cost you a deep belief or a reshuffling of agency in the process.
>
> A culture of Worlding—overflowing with annoying artificial aliveness—is the maturing response to a New Nature too strange and too interesting to ever be classically domesticated. Such a culture doesn't reduce the distance separating you from domestication. It feeds the distance as a feature of aliveness itself, and drags up habitability in the process. Such a culture sets the stage for the light of enchantment to keep burning more often in more people.

Ian imagines New Nature as a world of worlds where to live at all is to live in a state of enchantment in a condition of "annoying aliveness" via a pattern of exercise of agency that can be called "hallucinatory".

So far, so good.

Why is "annoyingly alive" (shades of *élan vital* there) the right description of this condition? Because even the smallest patch of reality isn't an uncontested piece of consensus reality turf you can "own" in any sense. Every agent can organize every piece of reality within their subjective perspectives, and have beliefs, desires and intentions concerning it. The world of worlds is not just hallucinatory; it is a collision of highly *opinionated* hallucinations. If designs and perspectives can separately be opinionated, designed perspectives can be doubly opinionated.

For instance, the character of Bikey, a sentient bicycle of modest intelligence but high ambition, turns the protagonist's walk into an eventful walk-and-ride by having opinions about everything. It is an annoyingly alive bicycle (annoying aliveness is a reliable trope for generating science-fiction comedy; *Futurama* is particularly full of good examples as is *Hitchhiker's Guide* with its Sirius Cybernetics products).

Even something as simple as a rock can defy simple existence in a consensus reality. At one point, Bikey swerves to avoid a crescent shaped rock. The protagonist picks it up. Instantly three other agents—a novel, a hypermind, and the character's mom (who are all wired in to the protagonist's consciousness of course), flow their narratives around it. Fortunately, these realities harmonize, so it is possible to reconcile physical possession of the rock with all three non-rivalrous intentions/attitudes toward it. Unfortunately, a fourth salient reality, the Soul of Los Angeles, does not harmonize.

These are alignments and misalignments. Alignments are valuable, misalignments may cause your reality to fork or collide with other realities. To live in a state of enchantment is to flow from one charmed knot to the next, changing scenes, forking, flowing, and standing still at exactly the right times, maintaining just the right evolving balance among alignments and misalignments to stay maximally, annoyingly alive yourself.

(Aside: While I was writing this post, I happened to have a chat about Stewart Brand, and how he's managed to craft a charmed life comprising a series of chapters that just happened to be the most happening scenes when he was part of them. That's what it means to live a charmed life in a relationship of enchantment with the world.)

Paraverses and Metaverses

I'm going to call the type of world-of-worlds Ian has constructed a *paraverse* and distinguish it from the more familiar term, metaverse. Para as in paranormal. Para as in a world-of-worlds sensed primarily through weirdness in the liminal adjacent possible around a subjective normal, rather than from an objective, outside-the-matrix perspective.

If your normal world is the coherent reality you think (or hallucinate) you inhabit, the paraverse is that normal world plus the contaminating weirdness that is a constant peripheral presence. It is a contaminated manufactured normalcy field that is always slightly nauseous[5].

A paraverse is a world-of-worlds revealed via the interactions of the experiential perspectives evolving within it. The world-of-worlds thus revealed may or may not have an objective existence and structure consistent with the paraverse. Ie, there may or may not be an objectively coherent metaverse "out there" that fits the experiences that constitute the paraverse. Every metaverse induces a paraverse for the agents within it, but the existence of a paraverse being experienced by a set of interacting agents does not necessarily imply the existence of a coherent metaverse at some hidden level of abstraction. There may be nothing to form a "true" picture of behind the scenes. It might just be an accidental theme park ride with no roller-coaster designer to credit for the experience.

If that's confusing, think of a paraverse as the viewpoints of the 3 blind men feeling the elephant. There may or may not be an actual elephant. It just might be a rope, a tree trunk, and a fan perversely arrayed in an elephant-like configuration of touch points to gaslight any blind men inclined to second guess themselves.

Or think of Kurosawa's *Rashomon*[6]. There may or may not be an actual "true" story underneath the stories of the wife, the woodcutter, the bandit, and the samurai warrior.

Or if you like philosophical parables, think of a paraverse without an underlying metaverse as a version of the allegory of Plato's cave where the operation of popping out of the cave, noticing the fire at the mouth, and recognizing that those inside are talking about shadows, is *not* well-defined. It's shadows upon shadows all the way out.

Paraverses are interesting because perceptions and experiences are the first-class citizens in the ontology. There is no higher category.

Unlike simpler world-of-worlds constructs, like a garden of forking universes constrained by some sort of legible, integral temporal logic (think time travel rules in simpler movies), or bounded quasi-worlds sufficiently separated in spacetime to only interact weakly (think space operas or monster-of-the-week narratives), Ian's New Nature is something like an evolving interference pattern of nearly co-extensive organizations of reality.

A paraverse is *maya*[7], and enchantment with it is the complementary concept of *moh*[8].

A paraverse is Baudrillardian simulacra[9].

A paraverse is a funhouse of mirrors and lenses, where even *you* are just a mirror or lens.

Should you believe in an underlying metaverse? That's an optional extra.

Paraverse Complexity

In New Nature, there's no birds-eye-view of whatever the hell is going on. Only worms-eye views from narrators who may or may not be reliable, experiencing reality through immediate sensory environments that may or may not have any materiality to them, while interacting with other agents like themselves who may or may not be inhabiting harmonized worlds.

A paraverse doesn't so much fork down different possibility pathways in a classical sense as pass through a double slit and interfere with itself[10], like a turbulent flow, but with quantum characteristics (ie, it differs from mere classical fluids like water in that information connections cause non-local entanglements).

It's not just an interference pattern, but an interference pattern of opinionated non-consensual hallucinations, governed by a rather anarchic collision of non-universal perspective-anchored rulesets.

New Nature is that process going on with such promiscuity and intensity that the metaverse level—if indeed it exists—is too cryptic to directly inhabit. So whether there is no there there, or the *there* is merely inaccessible, is a distinction without a difference. It doesn't matter whether a metaverse exists or not if you cannot go to it.

Here's an informal scale of complexity. Somewhere between 6 and 8, it becomes dangerous to assume a coherent metaverse level, and you're in a paraverse-without-metaverse regime of complexity.

1. Traditional mythologies (consensus metaverse)
2. Cowboy Western (+ procedural non-mystery adventure)
3. Hardy Boys mystery (+ procedural mystery)
4. Agatha Christie mystery (+ epistemic mystery)
5. *Rashomon* (+ unreliable narrators)
6. Neal Stephenson's *Diamond Age* (+ ontological complexity)
7. Iain M. Banks *Culture* universe (+ agency complexity)
8. Doctor Who, Discworld, MCU (+ coherent counterfactual/modal logics)
9. New Nature (+interference complexity)
10. Douglas Adams' *Dirk Gently* novels (+ ontological mystery)
11. Lewis Carroll's *Alice* novels and *Sylvie and Bruno* (edge of absurdity)
12. Monty Python (full-blown absurdity)

Despite its self-interfering complexity, however, New Nature as conceived by Ian is a plausible and realistic speculative future, since it doesn't assume any currently impossible technologies like time travel or hyperspatial jumping (some theorists might argue we've always already been there, and it's just getting too intense to ignore now).

New Nature does, however, create enough of an ontological mess at the edge of realism that it requires enchantment to inhabit successfully (without getting to the outright fanciful imaginings of Dirk Gently).

I'll save my comments on Alice's Wonderland for another day, but I've been reading a collection of critical essays on Carroll's work, and I've concluded that Wonderland is *not* a world of absurdity. It toes the line of absolute absurdity (a condition with no reality principle), in the sense of say a Monty Python world, without crossing over. To quote Harold Bloom:

> "Wonderland has only one reality principle, which is that "time has been murdered. Nothing need be substituted for time, even though only madness can murder time. Alice is only as mad as she needs to be."

New Nature is a place that stops short of purely fanciful invention and murdered time, and in a sense represents the limiting kind of paraverse where some sanity can be sustained. Only the mad can venture beyond. Dirk Gently is only as mad as the mystery needs him to be in order to solve it, Alice is as mad as *she* needs to be to survive, the cast of Monty Python are as mad as they *can* be.

Enchanted Flows

New Nature makes an interesting commitment that I share: *a paraverse is the obverse of a set of minds*. If the paraverse is a world of worlds, an individual world within it is an evolving coherent experiential perspective (or hallucination), accompanied by patterns of information and agency, *turned inside out*. Or what you might call an externally projected subjectivity. A hallucination consciously anchored in designed experience.

A world is a *point of view* that can impose itself on the material environment to shape it. A point of view is a stable stream of consciousness, associated with a (presumed continuously existing) mind that can be biological or artificial, embodied or parasitic, but is defined primarily as a self-perpetuating locus of responsive agency. This point of view can itself be "moving" in a general sense (ie acting under the power of its own agency, based on its own understanding of reality) or stationary. It can be a doer, or a watcher. It can span being and becoming, as it strives to impose itself on its environment. Success at such imposition is a feature of enchantment and annoying aliveness.

A paraverse is a set of enchantment-seeking dents in a metaverse, which may or may not actually exist.

In New Nature, there are worlds—externally projected subjectivities—that you create or author, worlds you inhabit as a participant, worlds you overlap or collide with, worlds you coauthor with others through transient periods of shared agency, worlds you observe but do not influence as a spectator, and worlds you can observe out of the corner of your mind, but not grok, worlds you align or misalign with.

There is a permanent traffic snarl worth of such worlds in New Nature, and they are all sort of at the same level of abstraction. They do not form a hierarchy that you can climb via progressively stacked conceptual metaphors and reifications, but that doesn't mean there is no temporal structure or ontological regularity to them.

The structure is created by the flow of particularly enchanted subjectivities. Just as someone driving through bad traffic, changing lanes and routes at exactly the right times, might "beat" traffic, there are patterns of (imitable) agency flow that can "beat" the paraverse and achieve high enchantment states. For a while.

The paraverse itself then begins to derive and structure its meanings according to the particularly enchanted experiences playing out within it. Just as the stock market is shaped by the lore swirling around the current cohort of successful investors who enjoy the enchantment halo of survivorship. The paraverse may be a traffic snarl of hallucinations, but some of those hallucinations are self-fulfilling prophecies.

In other words, our understanding of the paraverse comes to be shaped by the most enchanted experiences within it. Call this the Efficient Hallucination Hypothesis.

If Tennyson's idea of nature was about survival of the fittest, in a condition "red in tooth and claw", New Nature is about survival of the most enchanted, in a condition "blinding in mirror and lens".

[1] Ribbonfarm post *Meaning as Ambiguity*—Discusses how ambiguity drives meaning by allowing multiple interpretations, and how embracing uncertainty can enrich perception and dialogue. https://www.ribbonfarm.com/2019/08/15/meaning-as-ambiguity/

[2] The Euler-Lagrange distinction—http://www.tempobook.com/2013/06/24/lagrangian-and-eulerian-decision-making/

[3] The ergodic hypothesis states that over time, a dynamic system explores all accessible micro-states, making long-term time averages equal ensemble averages

[4] live player—https://medium.com/@samo.burja/live-versus-dead-players-2b24f6e9eae2

[5] Ribbonfarm post *Welcome to the Future Nauseous*—Introduces the "manufactured normalcy field," describing the nausea induced when rapid change outpaces our ability to make the future feel normal. https://www.ribbonfarm.com/2012/05/09/welcome-to-the-future-nauseous/

[6] Akira Kurosawa's 1950 film "Rashomon" depicts conflicting accounts of a crime, illustrating how subjective perspectives shape truth.

[7] In Hinduism, maya refers to the cosmic illusion that makes the world seem separate and hides the ultimate, undivided reality.

[8] In Sikhism and Indian philosophy, moh denotes attachment to worldly things that causes spiritual bondage and hinders liberation.

[9] Jean Baudrillard's "Simulacra and Simulation" argues that in postmodern culture, symbols and simulations replace reality, creating a hyperreal world.

[10] Ribbonfarm post *The Age of Diffraction*—Argues we live in an "age of diffraction" where information and identities split and refract across networks, complicating how we see and act. https://www.ribbonfarm.com/2019/05/30/the-age-of-diffraction/

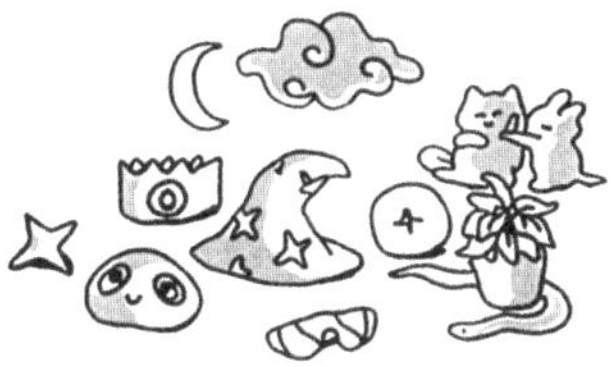

GLOSSARY

aliveness: the quality of self generating and/or self seeking one's own energy, especially in difficult environments. Vitality.

autonomy: awareness of the life scripts that guide you, followed by the choice whether to seek a new script or continue with the given script.

Art: a special kind of communication between artist and audience, for when familiar words and familiar forms won't do. For when you want to communicate something grey, complex, strange, or new, by composing together techniques, forms, symbols, materials that the mind and body can experience here and now.

Artwork: the mediating artifact crafted to convey the special communication.

Artist: anyone involved in the creation of an artwork. Used broadly in this book to encompass any creator who deploys some or all of their masks to their work.

complexity: that which cannot be entirely held in your mind, but that you understand coherently and can navigate to any of its parts. Prior to understanding, something complex is regarded as complicated.

compression: the transformation of noisy data into a pattern or rule that can reliably regenerate the data.

Creator's Hold: the degree of god-like authority the creator has over the World and its updates. The more permission the creator grants to others to contribute updates to the World, the weaker the Creator's Hold.

enchantment: a state of deep attraction to complexity.

frontier: Reality that is just out of reach for a World. The edge of a World. In contrast to home.

finite game: a game with defined rules oriented toward achieving a resolved end stage, win or lose. (James Carse)

flag art: art made with strong cartoonist influence. Symptoms: bait-like, meme-like, reactive, iconic colors and shapes, jokey, symbolic.

good art: art made with strong director influence. Symptoms: morality, narrative, mythological, historical, meaning-defining.

home: the comforting known protected center of a World. In contrast to frontier.

infinite game: a game where the only rule is to keep the game going. If the game is coming to a resolution, the game must change to keep going. (James Carse)

Life Script: the narrative map of a being's life. A familiar human script: "go to college, get a job, get married, have children, retire, die." A newer script: "first become a key, then go look for a lock." (Venkat)

mask: a coherent inner persona or pattern of thought that enacts itself through the body.

new art: art made with strong hacker influence. Symptoms: system/model centric, magic trick, wow factor.

New Nature: a name for Reality that includes runaway man-made complexity.

Classic Nature: a retcon of Nature: the state of Reality prior to anthropogenic influence.

Parent, Adult, Child (PAC): A model of human psychology developed by Eric Berne. "Each human being exhibits three types of ego states. (1) Those derived from parental figures, called the Parent. In this state, he feels, thinks, acts, talks, and responds just as one of his parents did when he was little. This ego state is active, for example, in raising his own children. It influences his behavior as the 'Parental Influence,' performing the functions of a conscience. (2) The ego state in which he appraises his environment objectively, and calculates its possibilities and probabilities on the basis of past experience, is called the Adult. The Adult functions like a computer. (3) Each person carries within a little boy or little girl who feels, thinks, acts, talks, and responds just the way they did when they were a child between the age of two and five. This ego state is called the Child."

portal art: art made with strong Emissary influence. Symptoms: alive, imaginative, unlocked door, governance, incentives.

Reality: that which, when you stop believing in it, doesn't go away.

seeking: the psychological direction a creator's mask wants to achieve: whether seeking a familiar and safe home, or seeking the unknown and surprising frontier.

steering: the motivational strategy that a creator's mask uses to maneuver around obstacles toward what it seeks: whether motivated by the immediate present (steering by gut), or motivated by the long term (steering by story).

World: a future you can believe in. One that promises to survive its creator and continue to generate drama. An infinite game that manifests itself in various finite forms, generates energy, and makes some part of Reality more habitable. Examples: an institution, a company, a country, a super-organism, a family.

Worlding: the art of conceiving, incubating, birthing, nurturing, and exiting an infinite game.

ABOUT THE AUTHORS

Ian Cheng is an artist living and working in New York. He has exhibited widely, including solo presentations at MoMA PS1, New York; Serpentine, London; Leeum Museum of Art, Seoul; The Shed, New York; LUMA Foundation, Arles; Light Art Space, Berlin; Carnegie Museum of Art, Pittsburgh; Fondazione Sandretto Re Rebaudengo, Turin; Julia Stoschek Collection, Berlin; and group presentations at the Venice Biennale, Venice; Museum of Modern Art, New York; de Young Museum, San Francisco; Moderna Museet, Stockholm; Whitney Museum of American Art, New York; Hirshhorn Museum, Washington DC; Tate Modern, London; Louisiana Museum, Copenhagen; Fondation Louis Vuitton, Paris; Sculpture Center, New York. Since 2012, he has produced a series of simulations that explored an agent's capacity to deal with an ever-changing environment. These works culminated in the *Emissaries* trilogy, which introduced a narrative agent whose motivation to enact a story was set into conflict with the open-ended chaos of the simulation. In 2018, he developed *BOB (Bag of Beliefs)*, an AI creature whose personality, body, and life story evolve across exhibitions, what Cheng calls "art with a nervous system." In 2021, Cheng directed *Life After BOB,* a real-time anime exploring human-AI symbiosis. Cheng is the founder of Opponent Systems, a new company building a social agent for kids and the family.

For more information about the author:
iancheng.com

Venkatesh Rao is a writer and consultant. He writes the popular Contraptions newsletter. Between 2007-24, he wrote the popular Ribbonfarm blog (now archived). He is the author of Tempo, a book on timing and decision-making, and is currently working on his second book, on the foundations of temporality. He has been an independent consultant since 2011, supporting senior executives in the technology industry. His work in recent years has focused on AI, semiconductor, sustainability, and protocol technology sectors. He holds a PhD in control theory (2003) from the University of Michigan. He is currently based in the Seattle area, and enjoys dabbling in robotics in his spare time.

You can learn more about his work at:
venkateshrao.com

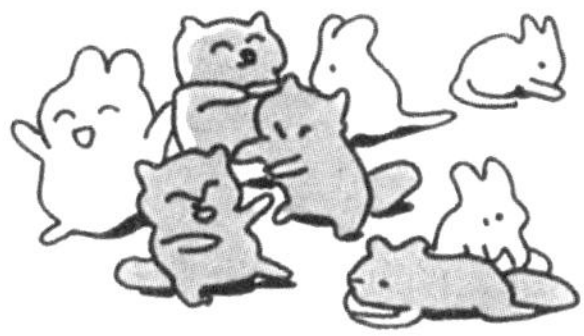

ACKNOWLEDGEMENTS

WORLDING: A Guide for Creators in Changing Times is a book that has gone through multiple stages of metamorphosis to arrive at the edition you hold in your hands today.

The earliest iteration appeared as a full-colour hardback edition under the title *Emissaries Guide to Worlding,* published in a limited edition on the occasion of Ian Cheng's exhibition at the Serpentine Galleries, London, held 6 March–28 May 2018. That edition was co-produced by the Serpentine Galleries and Fondazione Sandretto Re Rebaudengo, and co-published by the Serpentine Galleries and Koenig Books.

Later, Ian Cheng rewrote the original book for a more general audience, removing its direct attachment to the artwork *Emissaries Trilogy,* and releasing it as a standalone e-book under a similar title, *Emissary's Guide to Worlding.* This e-book was produced by Veronica So and edited by Veronica So and Nick Sung, with programming by Sixing Xu. Production assistance was provided by Claire Sammut. Support for the e-book was provided by Biennale de l'Image en Mouvement 2018, Geneva.

This brings us to the edition you hold today, published by cosmogenesis. This edition has been extended in format with additional material from Venkatesh Rao and Ian Cheng's exchanges on Ribbonfarm—as well as new reflections from both on the book and the subject of Worlding.

The author and publisher wish to thank and acknowledge all individuals and organizations named above for their roles in the development of this publication. They also extend their thanks to the following individuals, who at one time or another have been key to its creation: Andrea Lissoni, Andrea Bellini, Hans Ulrich Obrist, Kathryn Politis, Rebecca Lewin, Joseph Constable, Ben Vickers, Matthew Rogers, Silas Rose Cheng, Eden Rose Cheng, and Rachel Rose.